Improving Learning
in Secondary English

Geoff Dean

 David Fulton Publishers

David Fulton Publishers Ltd
The Chiswick Centre, 414 Chiswick High Road, London W4 5TF

www.fultonpublishers.co.uk

David Fulton Publishers is a division of Granada Learning Limited, part of ITV plc.

First published in Great Britain in 2004 by David Fulton Publishers
10 9 8 7 6 5 4 3 2 1

Note: The right of the author to be identified as the author of this work has been asserted by him in accordance with the Copyright, Designs and Patents Act 1988.

Copyright © Geoff Dean 2004

British Library Cataloguing in Publication Data
A catalogue record for this book is available from the British Library.

ISBN 1–84312–146–8

Typeset by FiSH Books, London
Printed and bound in Great Britain

Improving Learning
in Secondary English

Contents

Dedicated to my colleagues in the Advisory Team at Milton Keynes LEA, where I have learned a great deal about learning

CHAPTER 1

Some of the problems of learning in English

It is a characteristic of English that it does not hold together as a body of knowledge that can be identified, quantified, then transmitted. Literary studies lead constantly outside themselves, as Leavis puts it; so, for that matter, does every other aspect of English. There are two possible responses for the teacher of English at whatever level. One is an attempt to draw in the boundaries, to impose shape on what seems amorphous, rigour on what seems undisciplined. The other is to regard English as a process, not content and take the all-inclusiveness as an opportunity rather than a handicap.

(DES 1975)

Because there is no generally agreed body of subject matter, the boundaries of the subject are notoriously unclear and cannot be neatly defined.

(Protherough and Atkinson 1994)

Discussing 'learning' in English, as the two quotations above suggest, is an extremely difficult prospect. Yet, as the attention of the educational community is turning inexorably to a re-evaluation of and improvement in the quality of learning across the whole curriculum, English cannot expect to be excused from this examination. An attempt has to be made at this time to focus more clearly and 'draw in the boundaries, to impose shape on what seems amorphous, rigour on what seems undisciplined' if English is to be able to claim a full and valid place in the modern curriculum. Whilst the idea of regarding English as a 'process', as one of the alternatives offered by the Bullock Report quotation above suggests, has been attractive in the past, the 'learning landscape' of which English forms a part has changed. More has been understood about the actual processes of learning, and research into the nature of English (Tweddle 1995; Kress 1995; Morgan 1996; Lankshear *et al.* 1997) indicates that, despite all manner of attempted political manoeuvring, its main centres of attention shifted significantly during the last third of the twentieth century, but such movements have not always been reflected in schools. These powerful reasons make a reconsideration of what might be meant by 'learning in English' worth undertaking in the first decade of the twenty-first century.

There are a number of complicating factors in this discussion that require early identification. 'Learning' in English is not a straightforward business; it is not smooth, staged and linear, but 'messy', context-based and requires frequent recursive experiences. 'Learning' in English, in the understanding of many of those who teach and advise on the subject daily, is not restricted solely to *cognitive* considerations, but also has to do with *affective* knowledge. For some teachers of English, especially those with more experience (Goodwyn 2004), the affective or feeling understanding is of greater importance, whilst there are many others who would want to promote learning programmes that certainly maintained a balance of both approaches. There are also those who are just as concerned with promoting a sense of *enjoyment* (Pike 2004) to be experienced by the pupils in their English lessons, and who insist that such a response plays a necessary motivational starting point in any learning in the subject. These various, and sometimes conflicting and overlapping, interests will be given more attention in later discussion.

> English is a number of curricula, around which the English teacher has to construct some plausible principles of coherence. It is, first, a curriculum of communication, at the moment largely via its teaching around English language...this curriculum is coming into crisis, with the move in public communication from language to the visual and from 'mind' to the body. It is second a curriculum of notions of sociality and of culture: what England is, what it is to be English. This is carried through a plethora of means: how the English language is presented and talked about, especially in multilingual classrooms; what texts appear and how *they* are dealt with; what theories of text and language underlie pedagogies; and so on.
>
> English is also a curriculum of values, of taste, and of aesthetics. Here the study of canonical texts is crucial, in particular their valuation in relation to texts of popular culture – media texts, the 'fun' material children use in their lives – and in relation to the texts of cultural groups of all kinds...so...English is the subject in which ethics, questions of social, public morality are constantly at issue; not in terms of the 'right' ways of thinking, but in terms of giving children the means of dealing with ethical, moral issues on the one hand and by absorbing, and perhaps this is most important, the ethos developed in the classroom.
>
> (Kress 1995)

Possible reasons why a focus on 'learning' has been neglected in the past

It has been argued that considerably more concern has been given in the past in English to setting up and conducting 'teaching', rather than to the matters of 'learning' in the subject that any teaching was intended to bring about (Davies 1996; Barton 1999). Therefore, before I actually engage with ideas of what might qualify as 'learning' (itself a hugely complex debate, as we can already see) in this area of the curriculum, I believe it is worth devoting a short section of this book to examining possible reasons why learning has not been well-documented or regularly explored and appropriately foregrounded within the field of English teaching in the past. I am proposing this early diversion partly to help in the better understanding of this issue, and partly to establish more realistic starting points for taking effective action to change and improve upon the status quo. The following hypotheses, therefore, are attempts to make sense of a very complicated situation, and are not meant at any stage to be critical judgements about some very committed and hard-working professionals. My comments will be made on what, as a professional classroom observer and teacher trainer, I perceive regularly as a *de facto* situation, not on what should be or might be desirable.

The first problem is twofold: some people who are concerned with the teaching of the subject in a variety of contexts would claim that it is simply impossible to pin down all the considerable learning that takes place in English, about English and through English – and even when any learning might have been identified, to concentrate on 'learning' itself is to miss the point. Such an approach, they argue, would be likely to lead to mechanistic and limited lessons.

> Yet enjoyment is important too and is often left out of the debate about literacy...Policy-makers would do well to consider what makes 11–14 year olds *want* to read and write. Many teachers of English have long understood this and those with experience of adolescents are acutely aware that motivation is central to the achievement of our goals however egalitarian they may be. Any approach to secondary English teaching that focuses too exclusively on the acquisition of skills and does not take sufficient account of the human will and motivation of the adolescent learner is destined to fail.
>
> (Pike 2004)

Other commentators increasingly suggest that there is simply too little focus on the worth of what takes place in English classrooms – particularly in a period of considerable cultural and linguistic change – and the current situation has to be challenged and kept more immediately up to date. Whilst recognising and respecting many of the powerful arguments of the first group (and for a strong contemporary exposition of this point of view it is worth reading Peter Medway's 'Teaching and learning the English method' in the last issue of the *English and Media Magazine* (2003)), I am, nevertheless, positioning myself firmly alongside those practitioners who believe that careful scrutiny of the outcomes English teachers think they are bringing about as a result of their lessons is more likely to lead to greater success in meeting the needs of their pupils (particularly, but by no means exclusively, the least able) and lead to improved attainment for all. Jon Moss in his chapter 'Which English?', in a recent book intended for new teachers, makes the very same demand:

> As you begin your development as an English teacher, one question which you should keep firmly at the centre of your thinking, despite the temptation to abandon it which may result from your having to address more immediate issues, concerns your pupils more than English. What futures do you imagine for them, and how can your English teaching contribute to their development towards those futures?
>
> (Moss 2003)

Every day, in thousands of secondary schools, teachers engage with pupils in a subject called English. Those lessons have to be about improving the life chances, knowledge and overall abilities of the pupils concerned, otherwise they are not worth making time for. It is not acceptable that the young people involved in those lessons are presented with a collection of activities from which it is hoped, or assumed, that some improvements, positive changes or better insights are likely to result. Something of the shape and manner of the intended outcomes from those lessons must be anticipated and articulated by the teachers responsible for planning and presenting them, otherwise it will not be possible to ascertain how successful the lessons have been – or how well the real needs of those pupils have been properly met. If other progress, or positive personal change, or otherwise beneficial outcomes, not originally predicted by the teacher when the lesson was planned, come about from those lessons, then they should also be celebrated, and regarded as an important bonus. But the central core of what is intended in learning terms requires keen focus and attention, and must be properly understood by all the participants in those events.

Such a straightforward set of attitudes is not always apparent in the classrooms where English is taking place. It has not been traditional practice to declare quite so directly what is intended as the main learning outcomes of the various activities being put before the pupils. I maintain that there have been a number of traceable reasons why this situation has come to be the normal way of working in the subject. It is worth retracing some of the significant steps in the formation of the subject known as English, to better understand how the current tensions and positionings within those issues have evolved.

Early shaping of the subject

English professionals are keenly aware, day by day, that the problems suggested above are by no means new; they have been predicaments affecting any considerations in the subject from its earliest identifiable period. English, as most of us would understand it, is a relatively new school subject, generally agreed

(Poulson 1998; Mathieson 1975; Ball *et al.* 1990) to have first evolved into something like its present state during the 1920s, having been significantly shaped by the Newbolt Report, written for the Board of Education (a distant forerunner of the Department for Education and Skills), and George Sampson's book *English for the English*, both published in 1921.

> The Newbolt Report and George Sampson's book, *English for the English*, are landmarks on any survey of the subject's development over the past one hundred and fifty years... Both documents have greatly influenced later discussion about English in schools; they are still referred to with appreciation today.
>
> (Mathieson 1975)

Even at that early stage, quite different and mutually unsupportable tensions and priorities were vying for the greatest attention as the real core of the subject. On the one hand was the demand to provide basic literacy for a huge working-class population, recognised as being much less better educated than their German counterparts in a war only recently narrowly won. Gradual shifts had been made in previous years from the 'rigid rote learning and memorization [that] had been the predominant approach to teaching in the mid- and late Victorian elementary schools' (Poulson 1998), although most of the work taking place in classrooms was still based on fierce, decontextualised grammar exercises. A contrasting approach to the subject, however, was developing, as the direct legacy of the influence of Matthew Arnold and his belief that the only way to 'save' people from the morally corrosive effects of mass industrialisation was by learning large portions of great poetry. This belief in the capability of English, particularly English literature:

> as providing moral ammunition against an increasingly materialistic world was a powerful influence on developments in the subject. English at Cambridge and other universities in the 1920s and 1930s, under individuals such as Quiller-Couch, Richards and, later, Leavis, was influential in establishing the centrality of the study of literature within the subject.
>
> (Poulson 1998)

Attitudes about children and their potential for learning were also, however, changing from the sorts of perspectives that had prevailed for the most part during the late Victorian period. Less and less were they regarded as *tabla rasa*, merely blank documents on which to be written by the 'pen' of experience, or empty vessels waiting to be filled. They were, through the insights of educationalists such as John Dewey, being increasingly seen as developing individuals, with a potential creativity requiring the correct sort of motivation and encouragement to be properly developed. Sampson went so far as to claim that the English teacher's chief concern was 'not the minds he [*sic*] can measure but the souls he can save'! Alongside these developments, writers on the subject, such as Caldwell Cook, suggested a new sense of needing to meet requirements of pupils' emotional growth, causing a further, humanely liberal approach to the subject to be adopted in some classrooms. Yet another emphasis, urged by some small groups of teachers, was to regard the study of English as a nationally uniting force. Through attention to its literary heritage, and by giving focus to a supposedly 'common' language – it was thought – a hugely disparate population could be unified and given a sense of shared identity, however many different regional and class-based variants of that language existed at the time.

Frighteningly, the Tory government of John Major in the 1990s resurrected this notion of the subject as part of its 'back to basics' fundamentalism, at a time when potential political European union seemed to be once again threatening the 'English' national identity. In a multicultural age such a movement was, not surprisingly, seen to be quite impractical as well as ideologically unsound, and was quickly squashed. But advocates of such a position still emerge regularly, and often come to the fore when the school subject of English is discussed (usually negatively) in the right-wing press.

The social history of English – from secondary modern and grammar schools to the comprehensive

During the late 1960s and early 1970s, fundamental changes in schooling were taking place in most areas of the country: Circular 10:65, issued in 1965 by the then Labour government, heralded the way for the universal establishment of comprehensive schools, replacing the former tripartite system of grammar, technical grammar and secondary modern schools arising from the Butler Education Act of 1944. The teaching of English to grammar and secondary modern classes had been significantly different procedures since 1945, although both separate traditions can be traced back to both sides of the grammar/elementary divide which had grown between the two world wars.

For some years before, and shortly after the 1939–45 war, a large proportion of English teachers in grammar schools had trained in the tradition of the Cambridge school, heavily influenced by F.R. Leavis, and espousing his theories of a 'great tradition' of special literary works. Study of these texts apparently bestowed on their readers a 'protective' moral and aesthetic shield from the corrupting and destructive forces of popular culture. Such attitudes were a development of the ideas of Matthew Arnold, nearly a century earlier, so influential in one of the earliest manifestations of the subject. A fatal weakness of this approach to the subject was, however, that it depended to a huge extent upon an intelligent and already highly literate pupil population, possible to find in the fiercely selective grammar schools but not usually available to teachers in secondary modern settings. There was also little room in this particular curriculum for the creative exploration of pupils' own language use.

> For graduates from Cambridge and similarly oriented university English departments there must have been a problem in constructing the job as a pursuit worthy of such high-calibre training. The perceived low ability of many of the pupils appeared to rule out a definition in the grammar school tradition of the fostering of rationality. Yet the pastoral social-moral ethic of the secondary modern would not do either, since it was associated with low-status institutions and manifestly did not call for the qualities which English graduates distinctively possessed. The solution lay in the Cambridge notion of *sensibility* – that capacity for responding, feeling and living which all humanity was felt to possess in common. The cultivation of sensibility, albeit through writing and 'children's literature' rather than through great works, was an enterprise which was a) deeply worthwhile, since on it the cultural health of the nation was felt to depend, and b) commensurate with the capabilities of graduate English specialists since that criticism of life and literature which constituted their training involved the utmost rigour and discipline.
>
> In placing feelings rather than intellect at the centre of their subject, English teachers at the same time provided themselves with a democratic ideology which consorted well with the official aims of the comprehensive schools. Those emotional resources which in the secondary modern schools had been developed as a compensatory alternative were elevated to become the most important element in all children.
>
> (Davison and Dowson 2003)

The other contemporary approach to the subject, providing a very different context, that took hold originally in secondary modern schools and became firmly established in the new comprehensive settings, 'was based upon an alternative conception of experience and its relation to meaning, rooted in the immediacy of language rather than the traditions of literature' (Ball *et al.* 1990), and was known as 'the language in use', or the 'English as language' school.

> This critique was fuelled by the theories and research of James Britton and his colleagues at the London Institute of Education, and by the school experiences and classroom practice of members of LATE (the London Association of Teachers of English), people such as Douglas Barnes, Harold Rosen and John Dixon. The 'English as language' lobby sought to shift the canonical tradition from the centre of the English stage and replace it with the pupil, the learner. In other words to replace the emphasis on second-hand meaning, in the text, with first-hand meaning, in the daily life and authentic culture of the child...Here the English teacher was no longer to be a missionary disseminating the values of a civilization but an anthropologist mapping and collecting the values and culture of subordinate groups, initially the working class (later girls and blacks). The notion of 'literature' is profoundly expanded here to encompass all that can be said or written, to encompass language.
>
> (ibid.)

Those two opposing models were to set the pattern of attitudes to the subject for the period stretching from the 1970s to the present day. A crude stereotypical embodiment of these attitudes can still be seen today in the different starting points of the majority of members of The English Association and NATE (the National Association of Teachers of English – a successor of the original LATE), which could be regarded as, respectively, representing 'cultural heritage' and a mixture of 'personal growth'/'cultural analysis' viewpoints of the subject, discussed more fully in the next section.

Learning in English in more modern contexts

The questions about learning in English in more national contexts have been asked again and again over time. In cycles of about 20 years, there have been regular discussions – often regarded as 'moral panics' – about the (usually 'declining') standards of education that have engaged political parties, sections of the press and major employers' groups, and which have spilled over into public debate. At the end of the 1960s widespread discussion was once again underway about the sorts of developments that had characterised the period since the end of the war, as a consequence of the introduction of the Butler Education Act. In many parts of the country, local education authorities had effected the replacement of the grammar and secondary modern school structure with comprehensive schools, and there was understandable anxiety about the comparability of the new system with that which it replaced. English, and particularly the learning of language, always seems to feature prominently in such discussions. In 1972, a research study for the National Foundation for Educational Research (NFER), conducted by Start and Wells, pointed to the discrepancy in reading progress between working-class and middle-class children. This evidence was a sufficiently powerful catalyst to prompt Margaret Thatcher, then Secretary of State for Education, to establish a Committee of Enquiry, chaired by Sir Alan Bullock, to investigate standards of literacy and what was taking place more generally in the teaching of English. In its preamble, the Bullock Report (DES 1975) explored the range of approaches to English evident in the mid-1970s. As 'approaches' in any subject intrinsically point to what is expected to be learned from that work, it is worth noting what was going on some 30 years ago.

The Committee discovered that no one attitude predominated, rather:

> Some teachers see English as an instrument of personal growth, going so far as to declare that 'English is about growing up'. They believe that the activities which it involves give it a special opportunity to develop the pupil's sensibility and help him [sic] to adjust to the various pressures of life. Others feel that the emphasis should be placed on direct instruction in the skills of reading and writing and that a concern for the pupil's personal development should not obscure this priority. There are those

who would prefer English to be an instrument of social change. For them the ideal of 'bridging the social gap' by sharing a common culture is unacceptable, not simply as having failed to work but as implying the superiority of 'middle class culture'.

(DES 1975)

These attitudes are very revealing about the likely learning goals possible to be predicated on them. The first and last of these attitudes could, by no means, be claimed to be based on pursuing rigorous learning ends – we must wonder, particularly, what the learning criteria might be for 'growing up' and what they may have to do with English! The second approach suggests a very focused, but very narrow, view about the purpose of the subject, with learning ends that hardly lend themselves to promoting a broad overview of related language and linguistic growth. The report makes clear, as the quotation at the head of this chapter reminds us, that 'English does not hold together as a body of knowledge, which can be identified, quantified and then transmitted' (ibid.), and it goes on to suggest that there are 'two possible responses' to this situation: either small-unit learning 'through the medium of controllable tasks'; or

a readiness to exploit the subject's vagueness of definition, to let it flow where the child's interests will take it. Its exponents feel that the complex of activities that go to make up English cannot be circumscribed, still less quantified; the variables are too numerous and the objects too subtle.

(ibid.)

In retrospect, it is possible to read this paragraph as an 'excuse' for not producing clear guidance about the learning aims of the subject, but an equally valid alternative reading could interpret these words as being a condemnation of a woolly and undefined situation. Whatever verdict is made on it today, a climate in which the importance of 'learning' would be properly celebrated was not then in place, and such an interpretation would not have been understood.

Chapter 4 of the report, actually entitled 'Language and learning', offers the most important material in relation to this book. The Secretary to the Committee, Ronald Arnold HMI, who wrote the final published version of the report, is at his most powerful in drawing together and summarising the theories currently available about learning and language:

man's individual social and cultural achievements can rightly be understood only if we take into account the fact that he [sic] is essentially a *symbol-using animal*. By this account what makes us typically human is the fact that we symbolise, or represent to ourselves, the objects, people and events that make up our environment, and do so cumulatively, thus creating an inner representation of the world as we have encountered it. The accumulated representation is on the one hand a storehouse of past experience and on the other a body of expectations regarding what may yet happen to us. In this way we construct for ourselves a past and a future, a retrospect and a prospect; all our significant actions are performed within this extended field or framework, and no conscious act, however trivial, is uninfluenced by it. We interpret what we perceive at any given moment by relating it to body of past experiences, and respond to it in the light of that interpretation.

(ibid.)

leaning heavily towards the view of the London School, and its model of language relating to direct experience. The report also goes on to dispute the popularly held belief at the time that 'knowledge' exists independently of the 'knower', and makes a convincing case for recognising that 'knowledge' is what we construct from the past and what we expect to encounter in the future. It relates language and learning development in ways that has significant implications for the teachers of ALL subjects in the curriculum, and – whilst not being the first agency to suggest those particular developments – gave great weight to the notion of 'literacy across the whole curriculum' as a necessary topic of mainstream educational thinking. The 'language learning' and 'learning through language' positions it promoted were directly opposed to the traditional views of the teaching of grammar that had so dominated the subject in many classrooms until the late 1960s. Politicians – especially those on the right – sections of the media and traditionalists generally were deeply unhappy that the committee did not recommend a return to the sorts of 'certain certainties' of decontextualised grammar exercises, once the staple diet for the supposed improvement of language knowledge in most English classrooms.

The particular positioning of the Bullock committee was an important step forward, which has important resonances in our discussions about language and literacy learning in the early years of the twenty-first century. If pupils need to learn language in the contexts of the whole range of subjects in the curriculum, what will that language knowledge comprise? If certain areas of language knowledge will be acquired outside the English classroom, what areas of language knowledge will then be the province of teachers of English, and what will be ascribed to teachers of other subjects? What relationships will have to be forged about continuity and the best learning links between teachers of all the other curriculum subjects and their English colleagues? How will the school manage the overview of all language development? As Chris Davies commented on some of the issues raised by the Cox committee in regard to these questions, nearly fifteen years later:

It is meaningless to talk of a 'cross-curricular' view of the English subject area, or of any particular subject. The whole point – which the Bullock Report understood quite clearly in trying to establish a cross-curricular view of learning to use the English language – is that the relationship between the English subject area and the rest of literacy learning needed to be examined and developed.

(Davies 1996)

Whilst the Bullock Report had the intelligence and understanding to raise questions about the central dilemmas in English, it did not resolve them. The final published report was regarded with great respect in the English teaching community. Yet its effects, ultimately, were not long-lasting, because the disappointed government that had commissioned it invested no further in it, as the report failed to endorse a tighter attention to grammar teaching. For various reasons and certainly because of the lack of a clear sighted pedagogical view of English (always secondary to political considerations as far as any changes in the subject have been concerned since the late 1970s), the vital issues Bullock highlighted have not been in any way properly addressed in the period since its appearance.

There have, nevertheless, been other major opportunities to resolve the problems described above. The first tangible moves towards a national curriculum in English were made in 1984, under the direction of the then Secretary of State for Education and Science, Sir Keith Joseph. The HMI document *English from 5 to 16* caused widespread furore amongst English teachers when it was first published, leading to a subsequent set of 'responses' (1986), beginning with classic understatement:

> 1. *English from 5 to 16* caused a great deal of interest both within and outside the teaching profession … The document was clearly successful in promoting discussion.
>
> (DES 1986)

Many English teachers distrusted this booklet, as they believed it was a means of readjusting the priorities in the subject at that time. The uneasy compromises of literacy (embodied in the specific teaching of grammar), literary heritage, creativity and cultural studies, that had provided the backdrop to the subject since 1945, were thought to be in danger, with grammar having been manoeuvred by political means into a deliberately foregrounded position. The *Responses Report* (1986) highlights the considerable tensions generated by the original *English from 5 to 16* document:

> 37. Nothing divided the respondents more than the issue of knowledge about language. Colouring the whole debate were the experiences, recalled by many teachers, of exactly the old style of grammatical analysis headlined by some press reports.

Whilst not itself a document that had much ultimate effect on day-to-day teaching, the *Responses* pamphlet laid down the blueprint for more influential changes in subsequent publications. It restricted itself to discussing only the 'aims of English' as practised in English lessons, ignoring the 'use of English' in all other school contexts, thus missing, or deliberately ignoring, the lead offered by Bullock – a pattern that was to be repeated until the introduction of the Key

Stage 3 English and Literacy Across the Curriculum strands in 2001. It formally posited, for the first time, the levels of attainment expected of pupils in English at 7, 11 and 16, described in what it called 'objectives'. It also, rather more disturbingly, gave credibility to the study of English in four 'modes' of language: listening, speaking, reading and writing. Breaking up the teaching and learning of language into these distinct pockets of experience was to bedevil the organisation, planning and teaching in the subject for the next twenty years or so, until the present day:

> Whilst these four 'modes' ('speaking and listening' were placed together in actual fact) might have a certain validity in terms of general literacy, as clinically measurable skills which develop differentially, they are simply not valid as distinct elements of the English curriculum, to be taught and assessed in isolation from each other. Yet, as a result of this misreading of the Bullock Report, we have been stuck ever since with a means of organizing the English curriculum which bears very little direct relation to the way things are taught and learnt in English classrooms. It was a disastrous decision.

> (Davies 1996)

English from 5 to 16 also introduced the idea of 'Knowledge about Language', which gave the impression that specific issues to do with the direct teaching of language were being addressed, although, in actual fact, they were not!

The Cox Committee, the next significant agency charged with the task of formulating the National Curriculum materials to guide the teaching of English in all schools (DES 1989), also failed to explore what pupils should learn, but concentrated instead on what experiences they should encounter. Reading, writing, speaking and listening remained the organising principles, as modelled by the earlier HMI document, and the statements of attainment introduced through that publication were developed in detail for pupils at ages 7, 11, 14 and 16. The curriculum recommended by this committee was mostly well regarded by teachers, while yet again disappointing the government that commissioned it. However, it really contributed little new to the teaching of English, and in some ways might have done harm by setting in aspic many of the practices then current.

Yet, whilst not able to bring about much change to what it was that pupils should, ideally, have been learning, Cox and his fellow committee members suggested that they were aware of five broad approaches to English teaching, which they called 'views', the understanding of which can help to explain why learning featured so sparingly in English studies both of that time and subsequently. The five identified 'views' were:

- a personal growth view – focusing 'on the child' and its relationship between language and learning, and employing the study of literature in developing children's imaginative and aesthetic lives;

- an adult needs view – focusing on communication outside the school, preparing children's language needs for a working life after school;
- a cross-curricular view – focusing 'on the school', with an emphasis on the language demands of different subjects;
- a cultural heritage view – in which pupils were led towards 'an appreciation of those works of literature that have been widely regarded as the finest in the language';
- a cultural analysis view – focusing on the 'role of English in helping children towards a critical understanding of the world and cultural environment in which they live'.

These 'views' were not, according to Cox, 'sharply distinguishable, and they are certainly not mutually exclusive' (DES 1989). However valid they were as representations of English teaching – and they have subsequently been submitted to some rigorous critiques (see Davies 1996; Snow 1991) – they help to illuminate a situation where huge numbers of educational professionals are supposedly pursuing similar courses of study in a subject generically known as 'English', and very different outcomes and learning are expected to result from these unrelated programmes. Trying to identify and focus on 'learning' in such circumstances is an almost impossible task, and in respect of one of the most extreme manifestations of one of these 'views' – that described as the 'personal growth' model – any such undertaking would have been regarded as an heretical pursuit by most of the teachers adhering to that view. This is not an idle aside, as research by Andy Goodwyn (1992a) clearly shows. He questioned some fifty English teachers about whether they believed the Cox 'models' of approaches to teaching the subject (a) had validity; and (b) where each of those teachers thought they personally stood in relation to the five suggested categories. His findings were not surprising to those professionals in the subject, who, like myself, regularly saw English teachers in action in their classrooms, and had the opportunity to discuss issues about the subject with them:

> Cox's five models are recognised by a wide range of English teachers and his claims that they are generally present in English departments seems to be true...The survey confirms that the personal growth model, developed in the 1960s and 1970s, remains dominant.
>
> (Goodwyn 1992)

The grip of the 'personal growth' model of English

The 'personal growth' model was very much in evidence when I first became a local authority adviser in the 1980s, and was often the cause of problem meetings with heads of English and their colleagues. Left to their own devices in the 1980s, English departments had not usually devised guiding schemes of work to offer coherence and focus to different areas of the curriculum. Even some years after the introduction in 1989 of a National Curriculum, it was not unusual to visit English departments that were still resisting any suggestions that they might produce such documentation. Individual teachers, in the main, taught what they individually chose, although sometimes there might be common texts for specified year groups in the same school on which similar sorts of lessons were based. The outcomes depended entirely on what the teachers thought reasonable and manageable for each class. I was regularly informed by a few teachers that to 'impose' a programme of studies on their classes would have been tantamount to placing a 'restriction' on the creativity and imaginative possibilities for the teachers, and heads of English resisted imposing 'schemes' on their departmental colleagues for similar reasons. Teachers and their classes, the thinking went, would have suffered badly from such 'constraints', and 'English', as they understood it, would have been spoiled for ever by these mechanistic approaches. Chris Davies quotes a set of 'aims' of such a department in his book *What is English Teaching?*:

> We want our pupils to be aware of themselves and others in as wide a context as possible, both spatial and temporal; we want them to think, feel and communicate in ways of value to themselves and the community; we want them to 'follow an imaginative course, based upon the needs of adolescents in contemporary society, which will develop their intellectual, aesthetic and spiritual resources'. No attempt will be made to detail rigid schemes of work for the achievement of this aim. Every teacher is different; every class is different.
>
> (Davies 1996)

And this example, as I well remember, is by no means an extreme example of the genre.

Some of the potential problems about 'learning' in English being rather a remote notion in respect of the 'personal growth' view were actually described in one of the most explicit texts advocating that very approach:

> Certainly the swing to process has its own dangers. The first is over-rejection. If the conventions and systems of written English do not come in the centre of the map, where do they come at all? The answer is obviously complicated, so there is a temptation to ignore the question. Let the pupils spell or not spell in the orthodox style, punctuate or not, struggle with the ambiguities or not make choices of structure or not...it is up to them!
>
> ...The second danger...is the tendency to over-simplification of faith blundering from dull skills into the simple formula of 'self-expression'. Then the teacher can relax. Why trouble about people and things when the self is all-important? And, anyway, what criteria can – or dare – we use to assess what the self expresses?
>
> (Dixon 1967)

The majority of English teachers I observed teaching in those days were hard-working, committed and regarded the success of their pupils as their foremost responsibility. But any significant notion of 'learning' was not easily identifiable in that culture, either by the teachers or by the pupils, who would not usually have been at all clear about what it was they were, ostensibly, expected to take from those lessons.

As Davies comments on the above, not untypical, set of aims and the other similar examples he quotes:

> if learning is in everything then it might sometimes be difficult to know whether or not it has happened...If the broad content, the specific learning aims, and the teaching strategies all flow into one grand holistic soup, one ends up with the kind of long-term strategy – a sort of hope, really – that all these different learning events will just somehow build up into some constructive purpose inside the learners over time.
>
> (ibid.)

Caroline St John-Brooks, in her analysis *English: A Curriculum for Personal Development*, sums up the characteristic position of the time:

> the subject itself is, and has historically been, at the centre of immense ideological controversy. At the heart of this controversy is one of major value tensions in Western society: that between rationalism and romanticism. From the rationalist perspective, education is training for work, and schools are responsible for equipping children with skills to sell in the market place. Romanticism, on the other hand, sees education as personal development. So far as English is concerned, conflict can arise between those who see the subject in terms of the acquisition of literacy skills (spelling, grammar, letter-writing) which are needed to pass examinations and get a job, and those English teachers committed to what they see as the nurturing of human qualities vital to personal and expressive development.
>
> (St John-Brooks 1983)

Margaret Mathieson, in *The Preachers of Culture* (Unwin 1975) traces an historical background to this set of beliefs:

> From its beginning as two rudimentary skills (reading and writing) within the useful knowledge of the nineteenth-century's elementary school curriculum, English has come to be regarded as 'coexistent with life itself'. It is seen as the school subject which concerns itself with 'the personal development and social competence of the pupil'. Teachers appear to agree, in a general fashion, that the experience of literature, creative activity, critical discrimination and classroom talk constitutes the character-building elements in today's curriculum. The titles of three influential books – *English for Maturity* (1961), *Growth through English* (1966) and *Sense and Sensitivity* (1967) – suggest that English has come to be seen as central to children's moral and emotional development.
>
> (Mathieson 1975)

With such a large proportion of English teachers committed, historically, to the 'Romantic' starting point for their work (and a subsequent, 'follow-up' study by Andy Goodwyn and Kate Findlay (1999) confirmed that the majority still positioned themselves within the 'personal growth' model, although the 'cultural analysis' model had by that time, nearly a decade later, gained far more adherents than in the original 1992 survey), it might now be possible to see why any real emphasis on 'learning' has been side-lined by a great many teachers. How could it be possible to agree on any sort of realistic, clearly shared and understood 'learning' focus around outcomes such as 'personal and expressive development'?

More recently, the tensions of the subject, outlined in the preceding sections, have been exposed more brutally with the introduction of the Key Stage 3 English *Framework*, which many English teachers believe to be the secondary manifestation of the primary 'literacy hour'. The title of Andy Goodwyn's most recent research on the attitudes of English teachers to increasingly centralised programmes written by government departments, with no reference to the teachers concerned, effectively sums up the point reached on a remorselessly developing trend within the subject: *Literacy versus English?: A Professional Identity Crisis* (Goodwyn 2004). His concerns in the survey are:

> …the school subject of English, its high but controversial status and the battles that have been fought over its definition and control. The second revolves around what in retrospect can be called the 'rise of capital 'L' literacy' to a position of dominance. The third centres on English teachers as a professional group, chiefly as a specific subject group with particular, even idiosyncratic, characteristics but also as very generally representative of the erosion of professional autonomy of teachers of all kinds.
>
> (ibid.)

An apparently greater concern for teaching

The topic of 'learning' in English is not regularly debated or included on the agendas of the many meetings or conferences on the subject. Whilst hardly counting as a scientific study, a quick survey of books and publications concerned with this subject appearing during the last 30 years would soon reveal that much less has been written about the learning expected in English classrooms than the teaching which has taken place. English teacher courses and professional development opportunities specifically addressing the topic of clearly articulated learning have also been few and far between in the recent past. Disproportionate numbers of book titles have referred to teaching: *Teaching English* (1994), *Teaching Literature Nine to Fourteen* (1984), *Teaching Secondary English* (1993), *Learning to Teach English in the Secondary School* (2003), *English Teaching in the Secondary School* (1998), *English Teaching and Media Education* (1992), *Teaching*

Reading in the Secondary School (2000) being typical examples available on my bookshelf. Far fewer texts have the word 'learning' in their titles, although the authors of these named examples would doubtless claim that 'learning' is strongly implied in the fullest understanding of the word 'teaching', and, indeed, good teaching can only really have been said to have occurred where learning has resulted. But that implied or assumed belief that 'learning' is actually resulting from this teaching is the problem which *this* book is being written to highlight; because it is rarely raised or discussed very explicitly in the books published on the subject, learning has come in for too little careful examination. Incidentally, reading through the indexes of these subject-related books also illustrates that far more chapters inside those works are pointedly about 'teaching' than 'learning'. Searching the indexes of books about school-based English will also reveal many fewer entries of the issue of learning than of teaching.

At a part-anecdotal and part-speculative level, it is my clear impression that English teachers are often ready to adopt the excellent ideas and plans of others when they can, without spending too much time considering what the actual learning contexts of such work might possibly be – and little thought is given to what relationship the outcomes of such work might have to an already determined broader learning overview programme. Websites on the internet are full of lesson suggestions, and offer ready-made schemes of work, often gratefully accepted by very tired and overworked English teachers. As a regular course-giver it is very flattering to see the ideas that I suggest at such events being eagerly snapped up by the attending teachers, but I do try to stress that the small-scale schemes of work on offer are not free-standing, but can only fully make sense when framed within properly designed, broader learning contexts. Otherwise they become merely decontextualised 'entertainments'.

Failure to identify good learning in the national strategies

Nationally, this same avoidance of the issues of what properly constitutes learning, I would advocate, has seriously limited the raising of standards potential of the primary Literacy Strategy and the English strand of the Key Stage 3 Strategy. Those responsible for launching the National Literacy Strategy in 1998 were in a considerable hurry to get their initiative underway in the quickest possible time – to serve obviously political ends, before thinking through the pedagogical implications. David Blunkett, then Secretary of State for Education, actually promised to resign by a specific date if the pupil 'levels' of achievement had not been met through the adoption of the Strategy (although, in the event, he had, by that time, conveniently been moved to the Home Office). Unfortunately, insufficient consideration was given to how the 'objectives' they published might translate into classroom practice.

The preamble and introduction to the primary *Framework* document (DfEE 1998) outlining the suggested programme for teachers in Key Stages 1 and 2 makes 48 references to 'teaching', yet only six to 'learning'. This stance reflects the preoccupations of the authors of the document. They were determined to change the practices taking place in 'literacy' lessons, and to ensure that a large number of different activities were included, but gave little time to considering what the outcomes of those practices might be. So the *Framework* 'objectives' (a really tricky word in these circumstances, its meaning never fully made clear) are virtually all framed in terms of activities and, extremely rarely, in terms of what it is that pupils should learn, or be changed by, as a result of those activities. The beginnings of these 'objectives', on any typical page of the *Framework*, are written in the following ways:

> Pupils should be taught: to reinforce...to use phonological...to notice the difference...to read...to describe...to recite...to re-enact...to write about...to use rhymes...to make simple picture stories...to read and use captions...to read and follow simple instructions...to write captions...to make simple lists...to write and draw simple instructions...
>
> (DfEE 1998, Text level work – Year 1, term 1, pp. 20–1)

It is quite possible for the teacher to have 'covered' all these 'objectives', and the pupils to have encountered a very full programme of events, but have learned very little, or even nothing as a result. Not one of these 'objectives' has any suggestion of the essential elements of 'learning', – e.g. to know, to understand, to explain, to justify, to substitute etc. It is an outline that encourages much activity to take place in classrooms, but fails to focus on the essential business of how the participating pupils might become newly empowered by the changes through which they are now enabled to re-interpret and control their perceptions of the world. What they are to learn, ways in which that learning might be demonstrated and how that learning can be further developed are simply not sufficiently addressed in the current documentation. Most primary teachers, unfortunately, have not been alerted to these shortfalls, so their planning sheets are mostly a description of what will be going on in literacy lessons, and rarely, if ever, an outline of what will be learned as a consequence of the lessons.

The *Framework for Teaching English: Years 7, 8 and 9* (DfEE 2001a) is constructed in a similar way, and suffers from some of the same faults. In fairness, it is a much more balanced document in its references to teaching and learning: 'teaching' – or an equivalent word – is mentioned 34 times in the introduction, while 'learning'-related words appear on 18 occasions. There is a specific requirement to bring about, through the use of the *Framework* outline:

learning that is:

- active and highly-motivated;
- purposeful;
- creative and imaginative;
- reflective;
- secured in use and meaningful in context;
- increasingly independent;
- harnessed to personal or group targets.

(DfEE 2001a: 16)

which begin to reflect the sorts of concerns included in recent developments in 'learning' research, and are effective ways of framing the learning process, but can hardly be described as casting much light on the intrinsic language/ literacy learning process itself. The 'objectives' contained in the *Framework* are much like those of the primary counterpart document. Virtually all the Teaching Objectives are framed as activities:

Year 7

Text Level – Reading

Research and study skills

Pupils should be taught to: know how to…use appropriate…compare and contrast…make brief, clearly organised…appraise the value…adopt active reading approaches…identify the main points…infer and deduce…distinguish between…identify how…recognise how…comment, using appropriate…etc.

(ibid.)

Whilst a number of these words and clauses suggest what might be undertaken to demonstrate that learning has taken place, e.g. 'compare and contrast', 'appraise the value', 'comment, using appropriate etc.', teachers would, in the first instance, still need to establish clear learning foci. The document itself, however, as I shall show in a later section, fails to promote or model that essential preliminary approach.

David Hopkins, who currently heads the government's Standards and Effectiveness Unit, which has the controlling interest over the primary and secondary literacy strategies, is pursuing a policy of ensuring that greater attention is paid to learning in teachers' planning. Nevertheless, a huge opportunity was missed at the time of the publication of both of these documents to reconsider the issues of learning and introduce, at a stroke, a new national attention to it. Standards would have been better improved as a result, and many teachers, particularly non-specialist primary teachers, would have understood the real point and potential of the Strategy more precisely.

The questions of 'English' and how they affect learning in 'English'

Another huge problem to do with the subject, closely related to the issues discussed above, has to do with the nature of 'English' as a school subject. The word has come to embrace so many different meanings and interpretations, and there are so many depictions of the subject that any definition is in grave and real danger of becoming meaningless. Large numbers of English teachers, ITT lecturers, advisers and the senior managers of individual schools have great difficulty in defining what is really meant by the subject's name, in the manner of Medway, wrestling with this topic in the following passages. On the one hand he states confidently:

> the title 'English' is misleading. It isn't, mostly, as if the kids have to be converted from using some other language. Rather the job is to move students from less to more complex *uses of language*: the language in which we are able to do this happens to be English.
>
> (Medway 2003)

But after such a straightforward start, he then reflects the unease of so many who work in the subject every day:

> But we immediately see that this won't do without considerable qualification. Language is not the domain of English in the same way that living things are in Biology because English is about *doing* language and learning to do it better as well as knowing about it…What you come out of an English course with is not mainly 'knowledge' that you can write out in a test. Rather you come out able to do a variety of different things, having developed the linguistic muscles and brain–word co-ordination to generate a wide range of subtle and complex performances.
>
> (ibid.)

Yet, having pointed to some of the emerging complexities, he returns effectively to the really central question:

> English, then, is unlike Biology in not being primarily about discursive (stateable) knowledge. But, on reflection, to represent it as being about using language and not about content (apart from literary or grammatical facts) isn't right either. A lot of sentences are generated in the English classroom; they must be about something; and by no means all of them are about language. What they are about must constitute something that ends up being known about – or at least entering consciousness for a moment. What is that content?
>
> (ibid.)

If we could readily define that 'content' at this point, the rest of this book would be easy to write and instantly appeal to everybody concerned with furthering the subject!

So, what do we call 'English' to enable better learning?

All these 'sub-issues' of English, in their various ways evident in the original blueprint of the subject – and more (England, for instance, was far from being a multi-cultural society in the 1920s) – are currently alive in the myriad definitions and perceptions of the subject, and are regarded by different groups of its practitioners with different degrees of pre-eminence. So, at the end of the twentieth century, Rob Pope was still asking:

> Should we...speak of the medium of our subject as 'the English Language' (definite article, upper case and singular) 'varieties of English' (plural features of a single entity) or, more provocatively, 'englishes' (flatly lower case and plural)? When speaking of one of the main objects of study, should it be 'English Literature' or 'literatures in English' (there's a big difference). And in either case we need to be sure whether we're talking about canonical and/or non-canonical texts – conventionally recognised 'classics of Eng. Lit' or something else. Yet again, in a more challenging vein, perhaps we had better say our subject is 'writings, speeches, performances, films and other media in some variety of english'?
>
> (Pope 1998)

And he goes on to ask at the 'cultural level':

> Should 'English' be conceived primarily as the cultural heritage, even the property of a specific people located in or identified with just one part of the British Isles...in another sphere, do we hail 'English' as a conduit for high art and elite culture, or as a site where popular 'mass media' and other versions of culture can be played out? Finally (or perhaps first) do we see English Studies as a dimension of Cultural or Communications Studies? Do we align it with Humanities or Arts or Education or even Social Sciences? Or do we see it as a pervasively multi-disciplinary resource, as in 'English / Writing across the Curriculum' programmes?
>
> (ibid.)

These are just some of the fundamental questions that should be raised as a response to the main enquiry, 'What is "English"?', itself a reasonable starting point for examining what 'learning' might look like in the subject. Yet the sheer number of those questions serves to illustrate just how difficult any attempt to establish any popular central learning core might be.

One possible helpful step forward, suggested fairly regularly in the past, has been for the renaming of the subject, perhaps to call it 'Textual Studies', 'Cultural Studies', 'Language and Literary Arts', or 'Literacies', depending on the sorts of priorities society might come to regard as being the most essential – as if such a decision could ever be reached.

John Dixon very powerfully commented:

In England and Wales we know that 'English' exists – it's in the National Curriculum – but the code-word 'English' is like a polite fiction; it papers over differences. With the kind of conceptual fumbling typical of England, 'English' has been used as a cover term, to change things without appearing to change them, to allow the archaic to go maundering on. To understand what's happening under the covers, we have to analyse the struggles, political and intellectual, which they conceal.

(Dixon 1991)

Nick Peim, adopting an alternative post-structuralist position, challenges all the normal and standard expectations of the subject, to suggest that there are other ways of thinking about its content and practices:

Post-structuralism demands an awareness of the social, cultural conditions of meaning, of the dynamic interactions between texts and their contexts, the cultural practices and habits that determine the nature and directions of the process of meaning. Institutions – as organizing contexts – are centrally significant in terms of holding meanings in place, promoting specific meanings, enabling and disqualifying meanings. Institutions here include institutionalized reading practices, for example. Post-structuralist theory, then, enables analysis to go beyond the immediate encounter of reader and texts, and to come to an awareness of the culturally powerful, readily available systems and possibilities of meanings.

(Peim 1993)

Fleming and Stevens, in their book *English Teaching in the Secondary School*, attempt to analyse the problem of the title of the subject a little more deeply, and suggest why asking these sorts of questions is a worthwhile pastime:

What's in a name? you may ask, but thinking about possible other names will focus on what precisely the subject is all about and where the thrust of its teaching should be situated. Possibilities are:

- the language arts (favoured by Abbs (1976) amongst others);
- rhetorical studies (implied by Eagleton (1983) *and developed by Peim (1993)*);
- literacy studies (certainly in line with the present government's concern);
- cultural studies;
- communications;
- discourse awareness;
- language and literature studies.

(Fleming and Stevens 1998 (my italics))

– a list which fairly represents the main contenders for the current subtitles in the subject. Opting for only one of its many-faceted features as the agreed central focus of the subject, however, would have the considerable potential of deeply disturbing and offending those with a commitment to any other representation, that itself might not enjoy the same degree of importance or recognition in any new order. Yet, such a radical step will probably have to be confronted eventually, as a whole series of re-positionings in curriculum design and better, more widely shared understandings of the role of language in all learning will continue to impact on schools during the next few years. Realistically, however, for the time being, we have to accept a position where

> The point about 'English' as the name of a subject is that it is an adjective being made to serve as a noun. So 'English' is always pointing towards an absence – the noun. Is the subject English literature, language, society, culture, people?
>
> (Evans 1993)

Nevertheless, whilst any sort of wholesale reconstruction seems a long way from our current standpoint, English teachers should, as a matter of urgency, be devoting more time and energy to defining with greater precision what they mean by the term 'English', at least at local departmental level, and preferably within each and every school. Developments in Primary Literacy, since 1998, and the Key Stage 3 English and Literacy Across the Curriculum strands in secondary schools, introduced in 2001, have changed the modern 'English' teaching landscape irrevocably. These developments might appear to the casual observer to offer the basis of a fairly seamless transition, but the detailed reality is actually a more disturbed and potentially explosive situation. Many teachers of English in secondary schools are still determined to resist what they think of as a constraining 'mechanistic' approach to their subject, as it is currently promoted in most primary schools (Marshall 2002; Allen 2002).

Whilst primary teachers have, in the main, almost wholly restructured their 'English' teaching programmes since the introduction of the Literacy Strategy around the objectives suggested in *The National Literacy Strategy: Framework for Teaching* (DfEE 1998), very much focusing on a broad notion of pupil *literacy development*, their secondary English counterparts have maintained a distinctive centre of attention on literature and literary studies, incorporating in some instances features of sentence- and word-level work from the *Key Stage 3 National Strategy – Framework for Teaching English: Years 7, 8 and 9* (DfEE 2001a). They have, however, rarely established all their classroom work on the recommended objectives in the same manner as primary staff.

Neither of the documents referred to in the previous paragraph apportions much space to exploring what 'learning' could or might mean in the 'literacy' or 'English' classroom. Learning will have to be capable of closer identification and articulation if a sufficiently large group of teachers of the subject is to begin to engage in more consensual agreement of some of the main features of their subject paradigm. This discussion will be conducted more thoroughly in greater detail in Chapter 2. '"English" might be the best umbrella term for the time being, but the subject is rapidly breaking out from under that umbrella' (Andrews 2001).

Distractions from learning in English

English teachers could, however, rightly claim that they have gradually acquired a host of extremely good reasons for not regarding issues such as *learning* as amongst their most essential priorities during the past fifteen or so years. They have necessarily been wholly preoccupied in becoming familiar with, interpreting and implementing large packages of increasingly centralised directives setting out ways in which they are expected to prepare their pupils for a growing range of tests and examinations – few if any of which have concentrated on learning.

They have, in not much more than a decade, had to accept three versions of a National Curriculum and a completely new strategy at Key Stage 3; they have retrained and newly skilled themselves to cope with constantly changing national test and examination requirements for pupils at ages 14, 16, 17 and 18; they have grudgingly given disproportionate amounts of time to preparing for and submitting themselves to Ofsted inspections that rarely contribute to or benefit their personal, professional or departmental future development; they have been expected to meet growing demands from their managers to provide raised targets and improved league table positions, often in circumstances of difficult specialist staff recruitment, and with diminishing resources. It is little wonder that so many English teachers have lost the sense of autonomy that once afforded the sort of reflective and self-evaluative contexts in which identification of, and action about, central guiding principles of their work might be more realistically carried out:

> Teachers are ambivalently placed in the process of change. They are operationally central but strategically marginal; they have become accustomed to government generated innovation and acquired, through their participation in the drive to raise standards, new kinds of skill. Yet in terms of the management and direction of the school they are subordinate.
>
> (Jones 2003)

Many English teachers have expressed serious concerns about being asked to engage with creating sound pedagogical and philosophical backgrounds against which to place their work, at the same time as being bombarded with required approaches and end-of-key-stage tests that occasionally make a wholesale mockery of such sophisticated principles.

A clear sense of what schools really want to achieve in English

In 1984, when HMI tentatively published their booklet *English 5 to 16* (DES 1984) as the first in the *Curriculum Matters* series, they shifted the attention of English teachers from the previously distracting sense of the subject divided into 'language' and 'literature' to the 'four forms of language – speaking, listeni[ng] reading and writing' (although speaking and listening were actually conflated into one 'form'). They followed that introduction with the briefest of what we might now regard as outline 'success criteria' for each of the forms, and they are best seen quoted in full:

- Education in the spoken word should aim to develop pupils' ability to speak:
  - with confidence, clarity, fluency and in the appropriate forms of speech;
  - in a variety of situations and groupings for a variety of audiences, for a range of purposes of increasing complexity and demand;

  and correspondingly to develop their capacities to listen with attention and understanding in a similar variety of situations and for a similar range of purposes.

- In the area of reading the aims should be to enable pupils:
  - to read fluently and with understanding in a range of different kinds of material, using reading methods appropriate to the material and the purposes for which they are reading;
  - to have confidence in their capacities as readers;
  - to find pleasure in and be voluntary users of reading, for information, for interest, for entertainment, and for the extension of experience and insight that poetry and fiction of quality afford;
  - to see that reading is necessary for their personal lives, for their learning throughout the curriculum, and for the requirements of living and working in society.

- As to writing, the aims should be to enable pupils:
  - to write for a variety of purposes;
  - to organise the content of what is written in ways appropriate to the purposes;
  - to use styles of writing appropriate to the purposes and intended readership;
  - to use spelling, punctuation and syntax accurately and with confidence.

(DES 1984)

These descriptors of what, ultimately, a school or English department might be attempting to achieve for the majority of its pupils, through all its teaching and classroom experiences, are usually not given the attention they really deserve. I believe that it is absolutely essential that any group of professionals, working together in a whole-school or departmental team, should have agreed some clearly articulated overviews of what sorts of – in the context of this book –

readers, writers, speakers and listeners they are collaboratively trying to create. If the 'ideals' or goals of their efforts have not been agreed, then real assessment is very difficult to begin – beyond the skeletal mechanical criteria supplied in the form of attainment targets of the English Orders.

So, to 'define' readers, writers, speakers and listeners in terms of the incrementally developed stages of what they know – and to establish the means of demonstrating that knowledge – encourages a much tighter attention on the learning process itself. In *Teaching Reading in Secondary Schools* (Dean 2000, 2003) I set out the following reasons explaining why agreeing about the 'qualities or characteristics of a reader' would be a beneficial starting point for teachers pursuing shared attainment goals in their work:

> These principles or qualities are all capable of being separated into progressive stages or steps. They are all possible to improve, but no learner will ever 'conquer' any of them. There will always be something new to achieve, and continuing life experiences mean that every reader will discover more about reading...
>
> Teachers accepting these qualities as realistic strands of possible reading development should then be able to plan any reading work they intend with their classes as contributing to one or more of these qualities through all Key Stages. Policies for reading will be more firmly based on principles, not merely plucked from the air. Pupils made aware of them could be urged to use these descriptors and their increasing understanding of them as starting points for their own self-assessment.

What in that instance applied to reading could equally firmly apply to the development of writers and speakers and listeners. These recommendations are expanded and illustrated in detail in the subsequent relevant chapters on learning in each of the linguistic 'forms'.

Speculating about the future of 'English'

What takes place in the English classroom has, not unreasonably, regularly lagged behind the movements and linguistic developments of society at large. A certain time lag would naturally always be expected; all movements and developments do, after all, require a bit of time for consideration and evaluation to establish their worth, and there might well be matters in language change and the growth of new literacies that most interested parties in the subject would not want to see becoming a mainstream issue. Yet, the programmes in English classrooms required by law are so seriously trailing behind current applications of language and literacy in real life, the predominant interests of our times and the sort of knowledge that might be regarded as essential for a variety of users, that they are almost historically quaint! It could seriously be argued that the current English National Curriculum is more about maintaining the last vestiges and requirements of the

Industrial Revolution than about preparing young people for the blossoming Technological and Multi-modal Revolutions expanding at an unstoppable, exponential rate before our eyes. Only the slightest references are made in the official documentation to computing and computer technology skills, and virtually none to the possibilities of textual interaction made possible through widespread use of digitalisation. Certainly, the political interferences in school English studies, driven by strong conservative forces in the 1980s and early 1990s, desperately attempting to retain all that was saveable from the past in the teeth of huge and inevitable cultural change, did much to ensure that the subject was simply not in a position to respond adequately to the multiple 'literacy' demands of the beginning of the twenty-first century. Richard Andrews commented on the revised (for the second time in ten years) statutory English Orders published in 2000:

> Despite modest advances – and it will probably be generally acknowledged that this is a more balanced, more precise and more open curriculum than 1990 and 1995 versions – there remains the concern that the slow, lumbering process of curricular reforms is falling behind changes in the actual experience of language and communication in society...it is the result of a growing awareness that schooling and curriculum are losing touch with the real contexts in which learning takes place. The drivers behind the changing landscape for learning include an increasing access for families to multimedia and the Internet in the home; the gradual disappearance of the idea of 'education' as being a separate bolt-on dimension for cultural institutions, but rather it becoming a central part of their identity and function; a dissatisfaction among parents and children with conventional teaching techniques designed to gain maximum results for the school in its fight to rise up the league tables of performance, and changing literacies (e.g. the creation of websites by children and young people) that are not recognized within the formal curriculum.
>
> (Andrews 2001)

The notions of multiple literacies are not new. For well over a decade there have been conferences and study papers urging those concerned with policy-making in the curriculum, and particularly the curriculum in English, to integrate moving image study, the use of ICT and the potential of digital technologies into a worthwhile and stimulating English programme (Tweddle *et al.* 1997; Cazden *et al.* 1996; Goodwyn 2000; Bazalgette 1991). And the concerns of English teachers for these developments are not about merely remaining fashionable or appearing to be 'relevant'. They are intrinsically concerned with the nature of learning, and what sorts of 'learnings' might be essential in the immediate future to ensure that the changing literacies are understood by their potential users – and that they will be employed in creative and important ways in times not too far away.

Eve Bearne, writing in the UKLA research journal, *Reading*, in 2003, draws attention to the necessity of pupils being seen as readers and creators of 'multimodal' texts, where:

Shifts from the possibilities for literacy practices offered by the page (literal and visual) to the several dimensions of the televisual multimedia world, mean that children are being introduced to different ways of structuring thought. Not only are there now many more kinds of text to refer to than in the past, but also as children make meaning of new experiences, events and practices, they also think differently from adults' developed frames of reference.

(Bearne 2003)

Her arguments are endorsed by many researching and thinking in this area of development, including Gunther Kress (2003), Shirley Brice Heath (2000) and Elaine Millard (2003), who states:

Current multi-literacies are marked by a fluidity of movement between image and word, logo and logos, icon and command. Children become adept at locating significant detail on screen and moving effortlessly from space to space. Linearity is giving way to topographical awareness of the design of a page in print as well as on screen. Yet, children's and young people's increased access to the many varied means of multimodal meanings does not of necessity mean that they are sophisticated or knowledgeable about their preferences.

(Millard 2003)

Bearne concludes that we are still testing children through anachronistic testing regimes ('which greatly influence classroom practice'), constraining not only the manner and content of study, but also the thinking and learning potential of our pupils.

Rethinking literacy requires a pedagogy which can accommodate to children's situated text experience brought from the everyday world of communications and relate this both to the schooled literacy of the classroom situation and to the institutional practices which shape current practice.

(Bearne 2003)

'Reading' has for over half a century meant more than just extracting meaning from black marks printed on white paper. Film and media studies, only ever grudgingly allowed a tiny corner in the huge curriculum room of English, have been among those alternative textual foci making a case for the consideration of a far broader repertoire of texts as the fundamental literacy entitlement of all children. Similarly, digital technology has now made it possible to 'write' – that is to compose texts in fixed forms – in many ways: the capability for even small children to mix and weave still pictures, moving pictures, sound and written words into new texts with a range of potential meanings exists in most schools. These technologies are currently available, and yet they receive almost none of the attention they deserve in English classrooms, and their huge potential to extend and support ways of learning have largely remained unexplored. Still worse, we have failed completely to anticipate most of the implications of those devices quite likely to be introduced in the very near future. Hand-held computers, for instance, will translate spoken words into written text. What might be the effects on, and implications of, teaching handwriting and spelling in primary classrooms, with such inexpensive machines being readily accessible?

If those prospects seem a little too distant (and they are certainly not science fantasy), Andy Goodwyn reminds us that important questions should be raised about the provision currently being made in schools:

> I am concerned to balance the inflated claims for 'computer literacy' with the genuine potential for new ways of learning and teaching. Computers will not replace English teachers, but they certainly do some things better than any teacher; and they can, without doubt, improve the quality of our students' learning in English. I examine how teachers' attitudes and concepts are changing, how they are now accommodating ICT, and how this process is changing their view of what English both is and can become. Such a change involves a fundamental revision of the substance of English, viewing its nature more as a cultural resource than an inanimate heritage.
>
> (Goodwyn 2000)

The technology, like it or not, changes the nature of the work it is supporting and promoting, and will impact and change the important features of the subject itself.

The burgeoning collection of books and websites offering advice on learning, and exploring and explaining its nature for school leaders, all contain advice about looking, in a mature and undramatic manner, into the future, to make preparations for defining the sorts of learning which will be required for young people already in our schools, but for whom the future has not yet been in any confident way identified:

> There may have been a time when the world was static for sufficiently long periods of time to allow for a clear view of what skills and knowledge particular trades and professions required 20 to 30 years on. Such is not the situation facing our children today.
>
> (Bowring-Carr and West-Burnham 1997)

and:

> Although it is never possible to predict the future, there have been times in human history when people lived with at least the illusion of considerable certainty in their lives. In a rapidly changing world, however, this is no longer possible or even desirable. Educators can't hide their heads in the hope that 'this too shall pass'. They have a choice to make – wait until directed to change by others, or take charge of change and attempt to influence the future of schools and schooling.
>
> (Stoll et al. 2003)

Conclusion

Having reviewed some of the reasons why 'learning' has not often been the central focus of those involved in teaching and developing the subject, it is time to attempt an explicit argument about why the direction of previous trends should be reversed. Like Louise Stoll and her colleagues in the quotation immediately above, I want to encourage those concerned with English (or Textual Study, or whatever such programmes eventually come to be called) to 'take charge of change', and no longer remain the victims of reactionary influences and powers. English teachers in schools have been weakened, and in some instances wholly exhausted, by trying to keep up with the flood of directives emanating from central government during the past 15 years. Few of these directives relate to each other, and virtually none have much to contribute to what we would regard as important 'learning' in the subject. Most have been firmly posited on maintaining and extending an already discredited anachronistic curriculum, offering no vision of a possible or desirable future.

Not all the issues involved in these discussions lie in the hands of those who teach the subject, as Louise Poulson puts it:

> One reason for the continuation of debates is that the differences in assumptions and values informing different perspectives in English are complex. Furthermore, they are not always related solely to the subject. There are deeper underlying concerns which relate to wider social and political issues. At times of rapid social and economic change, which frequently undermines and challenges old certainties and traditions, language tends to become a particular focus for concern, because it is a key means through which people construct and represent social, cultural, ethnic and national identity. What is deemed more or less important in language and literacy gives an indication of the values and priorities of particular societies and eras. Ideas about the nature of language and literacy reflect ideas about which a society should function best. In the late twentieth century, the questions primarily relate to the ways in which English in the school curriculum can ensure that pupils have competence in the kinds of literacy appropriate to an age of electronic technology, and have access to the networks of communication within a global world economy. They also relate to the role of English language and literature in the maintenance of national and cultural identity.
>
> (Poulson 1998)

Nevertheless, it is time to reclaim control of the discussions about the vital purposes of English as they will be understood and needed by the youngest pupils entering the education system in the early years of the twenty-first century, during both the immediate period of their journey through it and then beyond, into adult life. Then, as a consequence of having satisfied themselves about what ought to qualify as the essential core 'learning' their pupils should encounter, and possibly transmitting a sense of that 'core' to those in power in government, teachers will actually be placed in much more powerful positions to take important and genuine decisions about what to include in their curriculum – whatever they are instructed to do by less pedagogically inspired authorities – because the rationale they are pursuing can only be challenged on good learning grounds. The professionals concerned with the subject should also find more common ground on which to agree and possibly to reclaim their shared territory in a way that has not been possible for some time. Divided, the teachers of English are vulnerable and powerless; united they could have great strength, but much more importantly, their pupils will have genuine access to, and take far more benefit from, the substantial learning opportunities such renewed interest and attention will have triggered.

CHAPTER 2

Why has learning in English become so important?

For many years, attendance at school has been required (for children and for teachers) while learning at school has been optional. In fact, in many cultures (including England, Canada and the United States), learning has not always been a high-status activity. Schools have been largely sorting institutions to feed a hungry marketplace. It is time to bring learning into consciousness and focus our attention to intentional and complex learning.

(Stoll *et al.* 2003)

In March 1994, while English Inspector in Oxfordshire, as part of the support role offered to schools, I published a small paper called *Revised Proposals for English: A Time for Reflection*. It is worth remembering that even though the National Curriculum had been introduced in 1989, it was not at all unusual to visit English departments a few years later that had still not been obliged to devise Schemes of Work or other guiding material to ensure a degree of greater consistency and purpose at any Key Stage. Indeed, some English departments thought me extremely meddlesome for suggesting such documentation. In the early part of the paper I offered a number of reasons 'for the necessity of articulating aims and intentions' in English as follows:

- unless a department declares what it is intending to achieve with and for its pupils, it will be impossible to establish to what extent it has been successful;
- only by knowing what the intentions are for its pupils can a department determine how it will devise a coherent and related system for assessing those pupils, the resources needed to achieve those ends, the Schemes of Work through which they will take place and methodologies and organisation required for their implementation;
- the teaching of English has changed and the knowledge now available about the way pupils acquire language skills and operate with language has become more extensive over the past few years. Linguistic researchers, such as Halliday; psychologists, like Vygotsky; and educationalists, like Britton,

have made important contributions to the way we should be constructing learning environments which offer the greatest opportunity for language growth, and there should be documentation to articulate such developments, reflecting recent research and scholarship;

- the teaching and learning of language is very complex and requires some explanation even for specialists, but certainly for non-specialists;

- English is much more than a practical communication skill, but the extra dimensions have only been hazily described in the past; the curriculum of the whole school is taught in English – what makes the subject English unique requires explanation;

- an important approach given fresh impetus by the Cox Committee and reiterated in the OFSTED Handbook for Inspection, is the insistence on speaking and listening, reading and writing as interrelated skills, about which pupils should be aware;

- what is meant by 'English', particularly in regard to English literature and its study, has been considerably affected by literary and reader response theories; these changes will need to be reflected in the aims of the department;

- English is only one part of an overall literacy curriculum which the whole school provides, other language and literacy development goes on across the curriculum: the two should be complementary and clearly shown to be so;

- few English teachers ever share exactly similar ideas about what should constitute an ideal English curriculum; published English departmental aims will only ever be a compromise, but they will, nevertheless, offer a collaborative consensus, requiring discussion and dialogue, ultimately contributing to team-building and the establishment of greater mutual trust in a shared ideology;

- recruitment and induction of new staff will be made much easier and more effective if departments have clearly established notions about the preferred contents and outcomes of their curriculum programmes;

- policies adopted by the department will be ineffective unless they are firmly based on shared, understood and published principles;

- challenges about the nature and purpose of the teaching of English are increasingly being made by different interest and political groups in society; a set of aims outlining the department's purposes will help to protect the team from attitudes representing only one point of view which might be directed against it;

- pupils already live in, and will continue to grow up in, a changing technological world, requiring new and different skills for an increasing

33

range of literacies; these should be understood and made explicit by the department.

I would claim that most of that material is just as relevant today, almost a decade after its publication, and that some of the points have taken on even greater significance in the intervening years. Yet the documentation articulating anything like a full response to the sorts of issues raised in that pamphlet has still to be discussed, agreed and written by most English departments.

Teachers of English have an overwhelming number of reasons why they should be completely clear about their purposes, and their core learning functions. Through establishing such insights they are much more likely to:

- have an articulated explicit focus to their teaching;
- bring about the means to enable colleagues to take part in more collaborative and developmental programmes;
- increase the involvement of their pupils;
- make their pupils more genuine partners in the processes of learning;
- most importantly, improve the attainment of their pupils.

The new focus on learning

Those concerned in the business of improvement of schools will not need to be told that during the past few years a major central concern exercising researchers and academics has been an increasingly distinctive focus on 'learning'. Louise Stoll, Dean Fink and Lorna Earl unequivocally make this necessary attention clear in the title of their book *It's About Learning (and It's About Time)* (2003), and they begin their text: 'In a fast changing world, if you can't learn, unlearn and relearn, you're lost. Sustainable and continuous learning is a given of the twenty-first century.' (ibid.)

Eileen Carnell and Caroline Lodge, in their book *Supporting Effective Learning* (2003), make their position utterly clear from the outset: 'Schools exist to promote young people's learning', and the 'learning' serving as the central word in this statement is not merely to do with the acquisition of facts. The discussion of 'learning' in this context is about learners – as a result of their learning – taking on new ways of considering the world and actually becoming changed as a consequence of what they have absorbed. This fundamental change to each learner is what Bowring-Carr and West-Burnham (1997) call 'deep learning'. They offer six 'levels' of learning:

A. Increase in knowledge

B. Memorising

C. Acquisition of facts, to be retained and used when necessary

D. The abstraction of meaning

E. An interpretive process aimed at understanding reality

F. Changing as a person

where the first three items can be labelled 'shallow learning' and the second three 'deep learning'. The first three could stand apart from 'me as a person' – they are the sorts of learning often associated with quiz shows and tests, and require little personal involvement. In the second three forms of learning, however, the person has to internalise, manoeuvre and rework what is known in new and wholly insightful ways, changing the nature of the learner – because that individual could never be the same again in the light of what has been refashioned.

Formative learning

In 1998 Paul Black and Dylan Wiliam, respectively the former and current Professors of Assessment at King's College London, published a small pamphlet, called *Inside the Black Box* (Black and Wiliam 1998), which has gradually taken on a huge transforming influence completely out of proportion with its size. This publication is the summary of a huge review of research into the ways in which assessment has the potential to contribute to improved learning. Outlining a host of government initiatives over ten years designed to raise standards of achievement, Black and Wiliam, nevertheless, return to a simple proposition:

> Learning is driven by what teachers and pupils do in classrooms. Here, teachers have to manage complicated and demanding situations, channelling the personal, emotional and social pressures amongst a group of 30 or so youngsters in order to help them learn now, and to become better learners in the future. Standards can only be raised if teachers can tackle this task more effectively – what is missing from the policies is any direct help with this task.
>
> (Black and Wiliam 1998)

They liken the inside of the classroom to a 'black box' – suffering a huge series of 'inputs', which are somehow expected to deliver improved 'outputs', without little real consideration of the processes involved taking place in that restricted space. By scrutinising the evidence of extensive collections of educational research, they invite us to look more closely at some of those interactions, to ask more searching questions relating to them and to rethink some of the practices involved.

Black and Wiliam are particularly keen to invite teachers to look more closely at the power and necessity of *formative assessment*. Such an emphasis is directly at odds with the government-sponsored insistence on *summative assessment*, which has been the dominant trend in English for about ten years. Certainly, since the mid-1990s, when Standard Assessment Tests (SATs) became the means of appraising all school children at the end of Key Stages 1, 2 and 3 (for children aged, respectively, 7, 11 and 14) teachers in primary schools, and the English, mathematics and science departments of secondary schools, have been expected to make judgements about their pupils' attainment relative to nationally imposed Level Statements published in the relevant National Curriculum subject Orders, and to submit those pupils for national tests. As a result, teachers have been more concerned with examining the difference between the current attainment of their pupils and the 'expected' Level they should be reaching at their age, than attending to the actual capabilities of those they are teaching and determining the immediate needs of those young learners. Summative assessment, therefore, serves as a 'snapshot', a quick check against a predetermined list, yielding a shorthand statement of attainment and numerical data, but does nothing to suggest how improvement and progress might be made, because it is a retrospective process only concerned with what has already taken place. Formative assessment, on the other hand, pays attention to the characteristics of individuals, attempts to explore what is within their grasp and where weaknesses exist, and points to the learning priorities for possible improvement. Summative assessment is convenient, detached, quickly administered and gives straightforward information, while formative assessment is demanding, requires close attention, the involvement of the learner and responsibility on the teacher for ensuring that the subsequently agreed required complex programme is properly provided.

A sort of fetishistic reliance on the National Curriculum attainment target 'levels' has been developed by many teachers of English during the past few years, at the expense of a much broader background of linguistic and literary progress. The eight 'levels' have even been broken down into 'sub-levels', so that teachers make reference to, for instance, a 'level 4b' pupil! This 'levelling' procedure was never meant to be more than a regular, but occasional activity, to ascertain where pupils stand relative to a few nationally published criteria, originally intended to be administered at the end of most key stages:

> The level descriptions provide the basis for making judgements about pupils' performance at the end of Key Stage 1, 2 and 3. At Key Stage 4, national qualifications are the main means of assessing attainment in English.
>
> (DfEE/QCA 1999)

English Officers at the Qualifications and Curriculum Authority (QCA) regularly state that the 'levels' should not be the only apparatus for assessing pupils' attainment, but their advice is not often heard. The dominance of a very powerful testing regime has, understandably, had a massive influence on teachers and their planning and, perversely, closed down and limited the assessment of the subject. Most pupils are usually judged by their attainment at the end of each educational year (because the culture of 'optional tests' at the end of Years 7 and 8 has now been fully established, alongside the Statutory Assessment Test (SAT) at the conclusion of the key stage in Year 9), and there has been limited consideration and development of a broad canvas of literacy and literary progression criteria.

Shirley Clarke, a researcher and educational consultant in her own right, has paid much attention to Black and Wiliam's recommendations and explored their effect in primary classrooms. Her powerful book, based on this direct insight into the potentially positive effects of formative assessment on children's progress, *Unlocking Formative Assessment* (Clarke 2001), deals with the following central tenets of this approach:

> Practice drawn from this research base tends to consist of the following:
>
> - clarifying learning intentions at the planning stage, as a condition for formative assessment to take place in the classroom;
> - sharing learning intentions at the beginning of lessons;
> - involving children in self-evaluation against learning intentions;
> - focusing oral and written feedback around the learning intentions of lessons and tasks;
> - organising individual target setting so that children's achievement is based on previous achievement as well as aiming for the next level up;
> - appropriate questioning;
> - raising children's self-esteem via the language of the classroom and the ways in which achievement is celebrated.
>
> (Clarke 2001)

Whilst Clarke's findings and recommendations have been mainly undertaken in primary classrooms, there is every reason to believe that they have just as much validity in secondary English teaching. I can confidently attest that they are just as appropriate in Key Stage 3 English settings, because I have seen for myself the undoubted improvements they bring about in classrooms where they have been practised. Their real benefits, however, are to further the promotion and development of learning in general terms.

Implications of formative assessment

Huge changes in the practices of English teaching could result from a widespread understanding of Shirley Clarke's work, based on Black and Wiliam's findings. The first matter on which considerable headway could be made has to do with the definition and adoption of clear 'learning intentions'. English teachers have long been familiar with the terminology of 'learning objectives', and have increasingly practised employing them as a way of focusing attention on specific issues they want their pupils to remember from their lessons. But the reality has often been rather too uncertain, and 'objectives' is a word with broad and unhelpful interpretations. The Oxford dictionary defines 'objectives' as 'an aim or goal', and teachers have become more skilled at anticipating what they are identifying as the central core of various units of work by their adoption of 'objectives'.

Semantic problems have blurred the full understanding and confident use of 'learning objectives'. It has been quite usual in the past for schools or departments to talk of 'aims and objectives' – as if they are different ideas. Yet, as the dictionary definition quoted above demonstrates, the word 'objective' also seems to mean 'a goal'. 'Aims', in this context, would seem to be that which is being regarded as the result or outcome of any enterprise, while 'objectives' would appear to be the means (activities and exercises) by which those results or outcomes are achieved. But such language has never been made fully explicit in educational circles, and merely assumed to be understood by those concerned with teaching in English.

> When discussing the place and purpose of objectives in English teaching, much depends on what is meant by the term 'objectives' itself, whether it is being used in a general sense to describe the purpose of a lesson (small group discussion and feedback on...) or whether it refers more specifically to precise learning outcomes (pupils will be able to...).
>
> (Fleming and Stevens 1998)

The use of the word 'intentions', however, for the same end, as used by Clarke, suggests an even closer specificity on tightly focused outcomes – it directly states what is *intended* to be brought about. Such specificity has not usually been a characteristic of planning in English, and leaves some teachers feeling uneasy; but it does enable those responsible for setting up interactions between teachers and pupils to consider more carefully what results their enterprises should be bringing about.

As discussed in the first chapter, there are too many instances in officially published documentation of 'learning objectives' not being to do with 'learning' at all. The *KS3 Framework for Teaching English: Years 7, 8 and 9* (DfEE 2001a) claims that there should be an 'emphasis on learning' (p.17) but offers mostly examples of teaching *activities* – e.g. 'compare and contrast', 'describe', 'acknowledge', 'recognise', 'identify' etc. – without ever modelling how those activities are expected to contribute to learning, or outlining the sort of learning to be drawn from these events. This is a very woolly understanding of the idea of learning. There is no sense of the learner 'being changed' – if we accept that idea of 'deep learning' suggested earlier in this chapter by Bowring-Carr and West-Burnham – through undertaking these pursuits. Teachers who have a clear picture of what they expect their pupils to be able to demonstrate as some sort of proof of their learning (which will come about through carefully selected, supportive and challenging activities) will then be in a position to share these intentions with their pupils, to enable them to become more effective partners in the learning process and not merely bodies on whom teaching is imposed. Teachers who have articulated what they require their pupils to demonstrate as some sort of evidence of their learning will also be able to express those same ends to their pupils – in the manner suggested by Shirley Clarke above (p. 37), to bring about more effective learning.

The practice of expressing 'learning intentions' (or 'objectives', as they are still commonly called) on the classroom board, or orally to pupils, is on the increase in many English lessons. Unfortunately, some of these messages are still not very explicit and a large proportion of them are, bluntly, not 'learning intentions' at all, e.g. 'to read a poem and analyse its meanings' (seen in a Year 7 English classroom in 2003); or the following, from a lesson for very able Year 10 pupils undertaking a 'non-fiction' module (sic):

Learning objectives:

- to investigate ways in which the injustices of 'globalisation' are presented in written reports;
- to gain awareness of the language of newspaper and magazine reports;
- to study the effects of emotive and factual writing;
- to gain practice in the effective structure of non-fictional essays.

Whilst I welcome the adoption of this sort of practice, there is still much more to be done to help many teachers understand what its true purpose can be, and the most effective manner in which such expectations need to be conveyed. Imagine for a moment asking any pupil in the Year 10 classroom quoted above what they are expected to learn from the work they have been assigned!

A few teachers, however, are making a good deal of progress in this area of development. One Year 7 teacher presented her learning intentions in the following manner:

Key Learning Intention

By May 21st you will understand how a 'recent author' weaves together the strands of character, setting and plot.

And another, Year 5, teacher stated:

Weeks 6 and 7 – Aspects of narrative

By the 17th October, you will know that there are different ways to open a story by showing me two different story openings you have written. You will also know that characters can be presented through different aspects of narration, including word choice. You will show me this learning by writing a new character or episode into the story.

Whilst these learning intentions could benefit from a little editing, the question put to pupils in this class about what they are actually learning in their lessons would be likely to yield a far more focused and clear answer than to the Year 10 pupils in the earlier example.

Involving pupils in their own learning

The work of Shirley Clarke and the recommendations of Black and Wiliam should leave English teachers in no doubt that learning can only be effective in their classrooms if the pupils are fully aware of and understand their own part in the learning process. Pupils cannot be expected to make progress if they are unaware of the goals they are pursuing, and that they are themselves full partners in the learning enterprise. Involving pupils in their own learning processes in this manner is also likely to ensure that the learning being formulated and intended is directly related to their needs.

These requirements mean that teachers have to do more than dutifully writing the 'learning intention' on the board as described above. It is becoming more common to find teachers sharing these intentions with pupils, but many such messages are not yet sufficiently focused to assist young people to concentrate on the central issues of what they should be studying, nor is time afforded to allow the learners to articulate *to themselves* what success in that learning might look like. David Perkins, in his book *Smart Schools* (1992) makes a convincing case to show how much more successfully pupils can be involved in their own learning when they can picture, or make clear images of, what their ultimate learning goals look like. Too many young people are asked to be engaged on endeavours that they simply cannot imagine, nor do they have an imaginative view of how they might transpire.

The real aim of this development in lesson planning and sharing, however, is not merely to increase the pupils' discussion about what will be taking place (although such discussion would be immensely beneficial), but ultimately for the learners to begin taking responsibility for shaping their own future learning programmes. In the twenty-first century we should be moving towards a position where learners of secondary age adopt a far more central position in respect of deciding and designing their own learning specifications, based on their perceived needs and preferences as well as those of their 'learning managers' or even 'learning assistants' (the difference is worth thinking about). Modern classrooms have begun, gradually, to move away from the 'one size fits all' model that characterised most twentieth-century practices, but there is still a considerable way to go.

Involvement of the learner in their learning changes the nature of the classroom from the prescriptive and directive to a negotiated participative and exploratory environment. In language-related learning, particularly, where 'learning about' also involves 'learning in' and 'learning through', it is necessary for all learners to have opportunities for relating all these various related issues. Research work undertaken in New Zealand (Jones 1986,1991) and in Great Britain by Neil Mercer (1995) also shows that pupils who are involved more closely in their language learning become not only more successful in learning language skills, but are also better enabled to see more clearly into the nature of language itself, and how it operates in what both areas of research call 'primary and secondary discourses'. Lankshear *et al.* (1997) sum up this overview, or 'meta-linguistic' position:

> It is more than merely knowing *how* (i.e. being able) to engage successfully in a particular discursive practice. Rather, meta-level knowledge is knowing about the nature of that practice, its constitutive values and beliefs, its meaning and significance, how it relates to other practices, what it is about successful performance that makes it successful and so on.
>
> (Lankshear 1997)

Progress in learning in English

Another reason why new and vigorous attention should be paid to learning in English is to ensure that pupils' progress is more effectively outlined, planned for, provided in language/literacy/literary lessons and properly tracked. Before the introduction of the National Curriculum, pupils in the different phases of education received a virtually random set of experiences – some more intrinsically language and literacy based than others – from the time they entered school until they left, and the majority of these encounters somehow qualified as 'English'. There was usually some degree of agreement about the content of the programme provided for pupils in what became known as Key Stage 4, those pupils in the GCSE examination-orientated classes, because it was described in the nationally shared examination syllabuses. Yet pupils aged from 5 to 14 had no such guiding overview to steer their curriculum. There was no generally agreed sense of what might constitute important 'linkage' or transition from infant school to junior school, or from junior to secondary school. There was not even, in the secondary context, any clear relationship between the programme of the first three years of that phase (what became known as Key Stage 3, Years 7 to 9), and the examination course which followed. And to this day, even with a

National Curriculum, that particular relationship of what should link these two key stages has still not been sufficiently defined in most English departments.

By making the claims I did in the previous paragraph I was not in any way endorsing the current English National Curriculum requirements. Indeed, I believe that the model imposed on schools in England has considerable faults and omissions, while serving some dubious political purposes that are little related to improving the necessary literacy/linguistic skills likely to serve our population in a modern, forward-looking age, or contributing in any valid way towards their leisure and pleasure. This despair with a curriculum not fully focused on what is necessary and possible for young people in our times has a long history. Neil Postman, the American media commentator, in *The Politics of Reading*, published in 1973, was similarly lamenting:

> As he [sic] is now provided with textbooks, each student would be provided with his own still camera, 8mm camera and tape cassette. The school library would contain books, of course, but at least as many films, records, video tapes, audio books and computer programs…Entirely new methods of instruction would evolve. In fact, schools might abandon the notion of teacher-instruction altogether. Whatever disciplines lent themselves to the packaged, linear and segmented presentation would be offered through a computerised and individualised programme.

> (Postman 1973)

Yet whatever future curriculum regime is imposed on English teachers, they will still need to have clear ideas about what constitutes 'progression' in the learning of the subject for which they are responsible, and applying a more mature attention to 'learning' will contribute to the development of those ideas.

If teachers do not share fundamental notions of what 'progression' in reading or writing or speaking and listening might possibly look like, they will find it more difficult to discuss what the necessary programmes, experiences or planning guidance should be put in place to guarantee that progression has genuinely been made by their pupils.

A consequence of the introduction of the National Literacy Strategy in primary schools, and its extension into Key Stage 3, has been the opportunity for primary and secondary teachers to talk together in a more common language about the relationships of their shared work. But this potential development of better communication has been very slow, partly because secondary English teachers still have problems coming to terms with these initiatives, and the perceived menacing greater emphasis on literacy and grammar at the expense of literary studies. Bethan Marshall, a teacher-trainer in English, who regularly expresses ideas about the subject which suggest that there was once a lost 'golden age' before the arrival of the national strategies, and who claims to align herself with the views of classroom teachers of English, was recently quoted in *Guardian Education* making this very point:

You have to ask whether anyone needs to know this, especially when it comes at the expense of creativity. We've reduced it (the English curriculum) to the level of linguistics, syntax and grammar and lost sense of its place as an art form to develop the imagination.

(Crace, Guardian Education 4.11.03)

Yet, the various National Strategies, as I have already tried to explore, will not of themselves offer the essential core elements of what might constitute 'learning' in English. Teachers have to look behind and beyond the recommended bank of 'objectives' offered in the two *Framework* documents to determine what they want their pupils to learn. This 'learning' is not the mechanistic sort of factual learning, such as knowing grammar 'parts of speech' to enable parsing-type exercises; nor is it the knowledge of raw biographical facts about writers, to be tested in a dry manner at a later time. The 'learning' I refer to here is about changing the learners in a profound manner, so that they genuinely regard their world in a thoroughly different manner after that learning has taken place. All subsequent considerations they make will have been profoundly affected by the learning, so the most detailed understanding of what that core learning ought to be really should take on huge importance and significance. Some of the problems of the Literacy Strategy development into Key Stage 3 have been related to the perception by a number of English teachers that the sorts of learning being promoted in the Strategy – e.g. the emphasis in writing on superficial issues such as 'adverbials' – have failed to qualify as learning of significance, and are merely readily accessible, 'testable' stuff, not sufficiently capable of leading to much real progression. I will attempt to examine the nature of that learning, and suggest detailed ways in which it can be furthered in subsequent chapters.

Increased pupil motivation and its effect on learning

Focusing on learning, not merely the levels that pupils might achieve, also has a significant effect on pupils' learning because research indicates that such an approach improves motivation. The Assessment Reform Group, following the work of Black and Wiliam (1998), surveyed the available evidence about the effect of testing on the ways that pupils respond to what takes place in their classrooms, and the degree of engagement they show with those activities. The ARG identified the sorts of actions that teachers could encourage to enable their pupils to be more readily involved in their work:

- Provide choice and help pupils take responsibility for their learning.
- Discuss with pupils the purpose of their learning and provide feedback that will help the learning process.

- Encourage pupils to judge their work by how much they have learned and the progress that they have made.
- Help pupils to understand the criteria by which their learning is assessed and to assess their own work.
- Develop pupils' understanding of the goals for their work in terms of what they are learning: provide feedback to pupils in relation to these goals.
- Help pupils to understand where they are in relation to learning goals and how to make further progress.
- Give feedback that enables pupils to know the next steps and how to succeed in taking them.
- Encourage pupils to value effort and a wide range of attainments.
- Encourage collaboration among pupils and a positive view of each others' attainments.

(Assessment Reform Group 2002)

Other reasons for paying attention to learning

More able pupils

Whilst any attention to learning must be capable of bringing about improvements in engagement and attainment for all pupils, it is also vital in any discussion about the fullest and most appropriate provision for those regarded as more able. Interest in these pupils has, thankfully, burgeoned in the last few years through such initiatives as Excellence in Cities, and other programmes encouraged by a government that has, at last, recognised that the needs of this particular group of young people require more specific attention. Yet any efforts by English departments to set up suitable and appropriate programmes for the more able in English have been hampered by the lack of clear understanding about what constitutes 'learning' and 'progression' in the subject. In *Challenging the More Able Language User* I made the following point:

> Only by articulating and sharing a clear sense of the way in which children grow and progress linguistically, and of what they might be capable of achieving, can the primary school or English department be confident of evincing the best from its pupils.

(Dean 1998/2001)

Developing these areas of greater insight and understanding are essential if schools are to get beyond the very limited 'more of the same' or 'harder work' provision still commonly carried out in classrooms across the country for pupils who display capabilities above the average.

I regularly lead courses for English teachers interested in changing and updating the ways their departments make appropriately tailored arrangements for their more able pupils. Yet, few who attend come from departments that have any sorts of published notions about how pupils learn language. They have not agreed on the ways that pupils might be thought of as progressing in reading, or writing or speaking and listening, beyond the National Curriculum 'levels'. It is not surprising, given these circumstances, that little proper accommodation has been made for these pupils in the past. I have never been able to understand how it is possible to draw up a learning agenda for more able pupils, one that is expected to challenge beyond the ordinary, without having already established a clear articulation of a 'first stage' foundation learning programme upon which any extension would need to be developed.

More able pupils in English have often been given more or 'harder' work in the past, as a way of apparently meeting their needs (or keeping them occupied). Yet there has been no real understanding of what might qualify as a 'harder' piece of writing, or what might be regarded as a more 'difficult' book, beyond the most superficial considerations.

Relating the learning of language and literacy in all areas of the school

Earlier in this chapter I suggested that a necessary reason for addressing learning in English was to enable more effective monitoring of pupils' learning through the school in lessons identified as 'English'. Yet those lessons are only a small proportion of the total lessons in the school where language is both employed and learned. Every subject of the curriculum is usually delivered in English (with the possible exception of modern languages, where many teachers mostly employ the 'target language'), and they all expect a secure knowledge of a range of literacy skills. While I would never advocate that an English department should 'service' the other curriculum areas, it is in the interests of all subjects that some sort of identification of the linguistic and literacy learning requirements are identified, understood and shared. As a result of this identification, all departments, including English, should be considering whose responsibility the teaching of such literacy knowledge should be.

These matters have been raised more openly in a considerable number of schools since the introduction of the 'Literacy Across the Curriculum' strand, as part of the Key Stage 3 Strategy since 2001. But much of the energy invested in this development has come mostly from subjects other than English, particularly from teachers concerned with the humanities, and a few teachers of science. English teachers have not, in the main, sustained their part in this essential discussion, and the broader subject-related linguistic demands have not been given much space in the overall English planning of most departments. In fairness, it should be realised, that these matters are actually dependent on senior management understanding and commitment. Only where a head teacher, deputies or senior teachers have insight into this whole-school issue, and are determined to address and improve this currently underdeveloped situation, as an essential aid to pupils' learning capabilities, will real steps forward be made.

Yet, English departments cannot expect others to take the lead on their behalf in this area. Teachers of the subject have to be aware of the linguistic practices and demands being made on their pupils for the majority of every week spent in school, if learning in this aspect of pupils' lives is being fully recognised and monitored. Pupils may, for instance, be competent readers of fiction, but not so confident with non-fiction, or vice versa. Such discrepancies should be known to someone in the school, because support and improvement must result from them. On the other hand, if a school has agreed a workable and worthwhile whole-school approach about offering helpful linguistic strategies to pupils, to enable their greater access to the whole curriculum, and to improve accuracy and greater self-esteem, the English teachers must have some sense of these approaches, and must incorporate them into their own programmes.

This changed mindset for the future is one that has not been easily achieved by many teachers of English. The realisation that 'literacy', not 'English', is the main concern of their work with the majority of pupils is still dawning slowly in some departments. Most English teachers have had only the sketchiest background in the actual teaching of reading and writing and speaking and listening. Most are immensely skilled in helping pupils engage with texts to discover different sorts of effects in 'literary' literacy; most offer supportive advice and help in improving certain aspects of written work and oral techniques. But few departments have a clearly articulated view of, for instance, what the *teaching* of reading might entail – and what they need to know about the background of teaching and learning of reading those pupils have already encountered.

Since the publication of the Bullock Report in 1975, the shared literacy responsibilities discussed in this section have been continually raised as a matter of great importance in many schools, but rarely followed through to effective implementation. Unless far more schools or, better still, the whole secondary education system takes this issue seriously, a major literacy learning matter will remain unresolved, creating a huge barrier to further development of English. The quotation from Chris Davies on page 10 reminds us that some formal relationship has to be established between the learning of language in the different subject contexts, and the relationship of that learning with what takes place in a subject called 'English'.

Learning styles and other related new understanding of assisting learning

There has been a huge flurry of activity in many schools during the past three or four years placing attention firmly on ways of assisting learning. The long-established work of academics, such as Edward de Bono, in relation to the improvement of pupils' cognitive potential has at last been recognised at school level, and teachers have been impressed with a range of ideas capable of bringing about more advanced thinking skills for children of all abilities. He has been associated particularly with suggestions of six 'thinking hats' (de Bono 1985), but others, such as Tony Buzan and Eric Jensen, have also written influential materials about emphasising the nature of thinking in the learning process. Alistair Smith is another leading exponent of the concept of 'accelerated learning'. This topic has been of interest in huge numbers of schools, and has led to considerable amounts of training. Teachers have also been encouraged to help pupils pay greater attention to the ways their minds work, to help them reflect more closely on the conditions and environments in which they learn most effectively, and to support their classes in adopting more conscious and reflective approaches to the tasks they undertake. Pupils have been asked to explore whether they have preferences for 'visual, auditory or kinaesthetic' methods of learning, in the recognition that we all incline towards certain environments that might not suit others. Many teachers now encourage pupils to drink water during the lessons when they want to, or provide music to improve the learning atmosphere.

Attention to preferred 'styles of learning' – the visual, auditory and kinaesthetic – has alerted many teachers to the different ways in which experiences can be designed to be introduced to their pupils. Too many classrooms in the past were passive learning environments, where pupils sat quietly and received messages from their teachers. A percentage of pupils actually can cope with being 'talked at', and they can readily accept what has been said to them, and make sufficient sense of it; over two thirds of the population, however, fail to absorb much from such presentations, and need either to see some sort of representation of what they should be learning (visual), or to encounter it, or make approximate contact, in some very close manner (kinaesthetic). So, a 'visual learner' might be helped into the plot of a play or novel by making a diagram of the characters or events. The 'kinaesthetic learner' could be better supported in the learning process by enacting, through drama or other related substitutions, situations or circumstances being explored. Recent observations in a large number of English classrooms suggests that teachers are offering a good range of different approaches to 'learning styles'.

Daniel Goleman has been responsible for drawing teachers' attention to their pupils' 'emotional intelligence', and the huge significance this understanding has in any overall learning programme. Put very simply, if pupils are not in the right frame of mind for learning or are distracted, for whatever reasons, they are unlikely to be successful in that learning, and any 'distractions' must be recognised and dealt with first. Also challenging preconceptions about learning are the theories of Howard Gardner, who suggests that there is enormous evidence that humans do not just possess one 'intelligence' but many, and that particular 'intelligences' might be better developed, because of genetic and environmental reasons, than others in each individual. So some people might be regarded as more able in 'literacy', or 'spatial', or 'interpersonal' areas of understanding than their peers, and such inclinations affect the ways in which learners approach their tasks. Andrew Pollard reminds us:

> Teachers meet the specific needs of children by knowing them well. It is thus right and proper that concepts to describe the attributes of pupils should exist. However, such concepts should be accurate, discriminating and capable of impartial application. Notions of 'intelligence' have a long history, but, given what we now know about the capacity of people to develop themselves, there are also serious dangers of stereotyping and inappropriate generalisation.

(Pollard 2003)

Yet another resurgence of interest has been evident in the recent renewed promotion of 'higher order thinking skills', partly, but not wholly, embodied in the research of Benjamin Bloom and his associates in the 1950s. The hierarchy, or 'taxonomy', of learning levels identified from this programme has been regarded as a useful framework for teachers planning lessons expected to bring about more effective pupil engagement and genuine intellectual interaction. The 'taxonomy' regards mere acquisition of 'knowledge' and 'comprehension' of what has been learned as commonplace, not much more than starting points in the real learning process, some distance away from the proper significance of gaining knowledge. More important than acquiring or accessing knowledge, are the ability and know-how necessary to applying what is known in some real-world context – so 'application' of that knowledge would be regarded as a 'middle order' activity. But far more demanding, and likely to enable pupils to make different and better relationships between their areas of knowledge and fuller understanding, are those opportunities when learners are urged to use their knowledge in contexts of 'analysis', 'synthesis' and 'evaluation'. Knowledge and comprehension, research suggests, are the staple diet of most lessons, whilst there is far less evidence of 'analysis', 'synthesis' and 'evaluation'. If they were considered more in the planning of lessons, they could contribute to the improvement of expectations being made about the rate of pupil development.

English teachers might practise a simple exercise in incorporating this 'higher order' thinking, based on Bloom's taxonomy, into their work. Using the framework of verbs, based on each of the stages, teachers could take a simple tale – e.g. 'Goldilocks and the Three Bears' – and consider the different quality of task relevant to each stage of learning. 'Knowledge', the recall of specific information, for instance, would mean being familiar with the plot; leading to low-level considerations, such as 'who was Goldilocks?', ''where did she live?' etc. 'Comprehension', an understanding of what was read, would ask a little more of the pupil; e.g. 'retell in your own words...', 'why didn't her mother want her to go into the forest?' etc. 'Application', where the pupil would convert abstract content to concrete situations, might be to do with the principles of the story, and lead to questions like, 'In what ways were the bears like real people?'; 'Draw a plan of the bears' house'. These are areas in which the learners have not had to make too much intellectual effort.

'Analysis', 'synthesis' and 'evaluation', on the other hand, require both much closer study of particular components ('analysis' – separation of the whole into significant parts), and wider thinking about the broader implications of, in this instance, the central narrative ('synthesis' – combination of ideas to form a new whole). 'Evaluation' expects the learner to make overall judgements, opinions and decisions, based on priorities, criteria and qualities that have been arrived at with considerable care. Therefore, 'analysis' or the comparison and contrast of the content to personal experiences, might give rise to questions such as 'How did each bear react to what Goldilocks did?' or 'When did Goldilocks leave her world for fantasy?' 'Synthesis' is the organisation of thoughts, ideas and information from the content, and might lead to considerations like: 'Make a storyboard of the events of the tale that does not follow its chronology'; 'View the story from the point of view of one of the characters'. 'Evaluation' is about the judgement and weighing up of characters, actions or outcomes for personal reflection and understanding. The sorts of questions raised about this approach might be on different levels: 'What might Goldilocks have learned about entering the bears' house?'; or 'Why might a grown-up write this sort of story for children?'

English teachers often use these 'higher order' devices, and 'analysis' could be claimed as one of the key areas of learning in the subject, promoted through all sorts of activities. Employing Bloom's suggested framework would fit neatly into many English study programmes, and would also highlight the advantage of demonstrating to pupils the different levels of intellectual activity they are capable of bringing to texts to enable better and more effective meaning-making.

Some teachers explain the 'taxonomy', or classification system, to their pupils and then encourage them to raise their own questions or tasks relevant to each one.

Verbs to associate with the stages in Bloom's taxonomy of knowledge:
Knowledge: arrange, cite, define, duplicate, label, list, match, memorise, name, order, quote, recognise, relate, recall, recite, reproduce state of, state, write
Comprehension: alter, change, classify, convert, depict, describe, discuss, explain, express, give main idea, identify, illustrate, indicate, locate, paraphrase, recognise, rephrase, report, restate, review, select, summarise, translate
Application: apply, choose, classify, compute, construct, demonstrate, direct, discover, dramatise, employ, illustrate, interpret, manage, operate, practise, prepare, schedule, show, sketch, solve, use, write
Analysis: analyse, apply, appraise, associate, calculate, categorise, compare, conclude, contrast, criticise, determine, differentiate, discriminate, distinguish, examine, experiment, find, infer, question, separate, test
Synthesis: arrange, assemble, collect, compose, construct, create, design, develop, formulate, hypothesise, invent, manage, organise, plan, prepare, propose, set up, write
Evaluation: appraise, argue, assess, attach, choose, critique, defend, estimate, evaluate,

Figure 2.1 Bloom's table of verbs etc.

These new areas of interest have, generally, been positive in the ways they have reminded teachers about the individual learning requirements of their pupils that should be noted and addressed in each class. A few of these methodologies have been adopted without too much understanding or evaluation in some schools, and they have not always been contextually based in a fuller learning culture that is capable of supporting and extending such initiatives. As John West-Burnham was heard to say: 'There are a great number of snake-oil salesmen currently at work in the "learning industry"' (West-Burnham 2003), suggesting a necessary note of caution before teachers rush too readily towards embracing them all. We must also note, however, that their promotion has been a direct challenge to the 'one size fits all' approach that has often marked the planning of secondary school lessons and the good sense of most of the ideas illustrated here are obvious to most teachers.

Professor Tim Brighouse, in a summary of what constitutes 'A Thinking School' (Brighouse 2003) on a website offers the following sort of checklist:

- Have the teachers, including the Head, analysed their preferred 'learning style'? Are pupils invited to self-assess their own preferred 'learning style' as a matter of course and to understand the implications?
- How does the school promote the musical, the visual, the kinaesthetic and the emotional (inter-personal/intra-personal) in opportunities for staff and pupils?
- Do teachers have a 'visual, auditory, kinaesthetic' element to their lesson plans?
- Is the assessment of pupils' work 'formative' and does it include specific and different targets for improvement? Have the pupils the tools (including target setting techniques and knowledge of learning styles, of accelerated learning techniques and of the next stage of their map of learning) to make progress? Are these included in the targets?
- What is the 'self-belief' programme for the pupils? How is it reinforced? etc.

(Brighouse 2003)

English teachers cannot accomplish these whole-school changes by themselves, or even in departmental groups, without the supportive ethos of the senior management and the determination of all other colleagues. They can, however, model the possible ways in which schools can improve, and the subject English lends itself to the trend of more personalised education that these changes are designed to foster. Greater attention to improving the learning practices of all young people in their lessons will be the essential first starting point for this desired change.

Having spent so much time and energy on suggesting improving the ways that learning can be supported and encouraged in English, it is necessary to attempt to outline what the stages of this approach might look in practice.

CHAPTER 3

Planning for learning in English

> English teachers often tend to conflate the subject content to be learned and the activities selected to achieve that learning. Such a conflation tends to result in a slightly bewildering looseness about aims...in the end it becomes difficult to distinguish what was *learnt* from what was *done*.
>
> (Davies 1996)

Taking time to decide what should be learned in English could occupy teachers for most of their professional lives, and leave little room available for the actual lessons themselves – there are so many possibilities from which to choose. Therefore it is necessary to have a number of starting points to provide a more focused and time-saving set of procedures. Certain current fixed parts of an English programme are not negotiable, of course. Since 1990, schools in England have been obliged, statutorily, to ensure that they include a required 'entitlement to learning' for all pupils, as a consequence of the introduction of the National Curriculum (DES 1990; DfEE/QCA 1999). This programme is a political document, and can, at best, be only very vague because of its necessary broad sweep, although at times there is irritating insistence on some very pointed and quite unnecessary detail (e.g. texts to be studied written before and after 1914!). The secondary National Curriculum Orders also outlines general cover for all five of the years of schooling, comprising Key Stages 3 and 4, with no indication of which parts might be better suited to certain age groups. So, while the current orders offer a framework on which a teaching and learning curriculum can be constructed, teachers still have to intervene to make huge numbers of decisions about what the many focused elements of their planning will be.

Since 2001, secondary teachers have been further supported (or challenged, depending on one's point of view) in these decision-making processes by being encouraged to embed in their approaches the 'objectives' from a *Framework for Teaching* for pupils in years 7 to 9 (DfEE 2001a). Whilst this document has offered guidance in drawing together different sorts of study in a more systematic way – e.g. in Years 7, 8 and 9 pupils are expected to undertake study, year on year, in 'understanding the author's craft', and be taught writing skills that 'imagine, explore and entertain' for those year groups – offering some developmental shaping and the chance for devising a sense of 'progression', much ultimate decision-making about the actual content is still left to individual departments when setting up their teaching and learning syllabus.

The course outline for English in Key Stage 4 has traditionally been much easier for schools to organise, as it has usually been based solidly and undeviatingly on the GCSE examination syllabus. In the past this was a very simple arrangement; there was one examination called 'English language' that tested broad literacy skills, such as 'reading comprehension' and 'essay writing', alongside, possibly, the composition of a piece of narrative. For those pupils with more confident reading and writing abilities, a further examination was available, called 'English literature', testing knowledge and simple analysis of the meanings of prose, poetry and drama texts. During the last decade, however, there has been a curious morphing of the two formerly distinct papers, to the extent that it is currently difficult to differentiate one from the other, in a manner that rather crudely parodies some of the confusions currently inherent in the subject.

Nevertheless, most English departments have tended to regard the programmes in Key Stages 3 and 4 as separate entities. Certainly teachers have expected the fundamental reading and writing skills (particularly the secretarial elements of writing) encouraged and honed in Years 7 to 9 to be employed with full confidence in Key Stage 4, but more significant text-level learning has not traditionally been planned and taught in the junior years, to be drawn on and developed in Years 10 and 11.

Paradoxically, there is considerable study of texts in most Key Stage 3 classes, but the vast proportion of that study is 'self-contained'; about and centred on individual texts; i.e. a novel, a collection of poems or play is read, meanings are sought and some analysis takes place providing a model for similar study, but that selected novel, poetry collection or play is not approached as a characteristic example of a genre, or movement, or literary trend, or of having some notable relationship with other texts containing similar (or contrasting) qualities produced in a similar period, or for similar/opposing purposes.

So it is usual in current circumstances to visit Year 7 English lessons, where pupils are reading and studying, for instance, a universally popular novel by the American author Louis Sacher, called *Holes*, published in 1998. The class will consider the unfolding and linking of interweaving plots, the coincidences that make the novel so intriguing, the characters and settings – and possibly a few aspects of the language. They might write 'letters' from characters in the novel to others or compose 'diaries' of the inmates of Camp Green Lake or 'wanted' posters of Kissin' Kate Barlow. Rarely, however, will they be encouraged to place *Holes* into an historic literary context, to see it as a good example of the postmodern novel, with its characteristics of magic realism, very different from the social realist narratives of an earlier time, such as *Of Mice and Men*. The too-focused centre of study provided by this model of teaching gives few opportunities for 'learning' about whole varieties and sorts of texts, and offers pupils little opportunity to make intellectual relationships about 'communities of texts' – or any important way in which to relate such a novel to other novels (as an example of one form of text) in general.

In a paper written for the National Literacy Strategy, Shirley Clarke comments: 'There is still a need to sort out learning intentions at the planning stage. Too many learning intentions are in fact activities and *contain the context of the learning*' (Clarke 2003). The example I have given above illustrates this problem, which is not one that seems to have exercised or disturbed many English teachers in the past. The novel *Holes* is merely the 'context' for learning. It is not, and never could be, of itself, the learning intention. The key learning intention of any study of *Holes* will not be 'to know the novel called *Holes*'. Instead, teachers have to begin thinking in terms of 'What learning do I want to employ this text to illustrate or to demonstrate, that these pupils should know and be able to use in other encounters with similar texts in similar contexts?'

'Contexts', as Shirley Clarke defines them, have tended to be the organising mechanism of many English programmes of study. It is quite usual to see these different 'contexts' separately, placed alongside each other as the syllabus for every year group, thus becoming the units of work of the department. Unfortunately, because the 'units' in which these 'contexts' take place are themselves dealt with quite distinctively, and the content of the 'units' are so equally introspective, all opportunity for real 'progression' possible to be pursued through these stages is lost. Departments do not exploit the available time in Key Stage 3 in the fullest positive way to ensure that the significant learning issues, so necessary for success in the examinations that conclude Key Stage 4, are introduced and can be built upon systematically. All the necessary parts of the study programme may be included, but a proper sense of what real overall progress might mean has not been identified and is therefore impossible to track systematically.

I am in possible danger of getting ahead of myself by using these sorts of examples at this time, but I believe that it is necessary to challenge the ways that texts are employed in English classrooms if I am going to change the approaches to planning that have dominated work in the subject in the past. Therefore, I have tried to explore, with a well-known example, the assumptions that currently steer teachers in their procedures, as a means of suggesting that a new set of guiding principles need to be in place if any real alternatives are to gain any real foothold.

What 'learning in English' could mean

There is little point in suggesting to English teachers that they should consider changing their approaches to planning and how they might prepare different sorts of learning programmes for their pupils without actually offering a notion of what 'learning' in the subject might look like. I would like to offer the following ideas as a starting point for further investigation and articulation:

Characteristics of good learning and progress in English/literacy

Good learning in English should enable learners independently to make the fullest range of meanings from the broadest possible range of textual engagements (through listening and reading in its many interpretations), and to express the most appropriate, relevant and effective meanings in texts being constructed (through speaking and writing in all available media), and to recognise how those meanings relate to the forms and media in which they are conveyed.

Where learners are learning English/literacy effectively they:

- are clear about the purposes of texts, and understand how their forms and linguistic and meaning-making structures and devices fulfil those purposes;
- are fully aware of how texts have effects on their audiences;
- are able to relate texts with the contexts in which they were constructed, and the agencies responsible for them;
- are increasingly able to deconstruct, analyse and make meanings with texts, and to use those understandings to construct appropriate, purposeful and accurate texts of their own for a growing variety of purposes and audiences;
- are increasingly able to articulate their own developing responses to, enjoyment of and reasons for making a wide range of contextual choices in respect of an ever-growing variety of textual materials;
- are aware that all textual materials contain the potential for further creative textual construction and adaptation;
- are able to listen to, and read with greater critical attention, a growing range of discourses and to make more confident, appropriate and accurate spoken or written responses in a growing range of contexts;
- are familiar with a wide range of literary arts and their relationships with other art forms;
- are knowledgeable about the potential of language to support and develop

learning and thinking, and to define and express power, gender, personal and other social relationships;

- pay more reflective critical attention to, and strive to improve, their own appropriate and accurate use of language in the widest possible available contexts.

Good learning in English/literacy also enables learners to:

- know more of the cultural traditions and contexts in which texts have been devised, the values they contain and the range of possible relationships between author and audience;
- understand how language changes over time;
- use and employ reference and other ostensibly devised learning materials in a range of media more skilfully;
- develop greater powers of empathy and the understanding of how others feel and respond in a variety of situations;
- understand how to evaluate their own strengths and weaknesses, and to know the ways in which to make improvement;
- know that learning language and wanting to conduct exploration of its possible uses is a lifelong process.

This good learning focus will have come about from a confident sense of secure teaching practices, such as the following:

Characteristics of good teaching specific to English/literacy

- clear and accurate awareness of the learner's current capabilities, attainment and interests as the starting point for further learning, through appropriately challenging activities leading to worthwhile new stages of learning;
- the understanding that effective literacy/literary development comes about through study of authentic, purposeful textual materials devised for real audiences;
- well-paced, well-structured activities leading to practice and consolidation of learning, properly understood and articulated by teachers and learners, in the widest possible range of appropriate contexts;
- opportunities for learners to take the initiative in realistic social situations as contexts in which to develop more extended, complex and sophisticated purposeful responses;

- effective feedback to learners about their own meaning-making and meaning construction engagements and strategies to bring about continuing improvement;

- good modelling of deconstruction, analytical and compositional skills, to enable pupils to become increasingly independent in applying them to textual engagements for their own purposes;

- acquainting learners with the widest possible range of textual materials, in all available media, to enable the making of the fullest associations between them;

- regular reflection on the learning that has occurred, to bring about the development of skills of self-improvement.

This exact form of words will possibly not be the most popular way of expressing what teachers of English (and literacy) believe are their main purposes, but I offer them as the starting point of an essential discussion. It is time to bear in mind that English and literacy are inextricably linked, and that the literacy element should no longer merely be assumed in any discussion of the subject, but emphasised very obviously. If English departments are to address fully issues of learning in the future, they will have to begin thinking in the manner modelled above. From the moment English teachers begin answering questions, such as 'What are the core areas of *learning* that we must establish for all pupils?', they will find themselves thinking in the sorts of terms suggested above. If those terms are then also placed alongside definitions of what a 'reader', 'writer', 'speaker' and 'listener' should be – or, at least, the sorts of 'reader', 'writer', 'speaker' and 'listener' the school is striving to bring about as a result of its learning programme – then planning will become a far more directed and focused process.

The vocabulary of learning

Research shows that children are more motivated and task-oriented if they know the learning intentions of the task, but they are also able to make better decisions about *how to go about the task*. Without the learning intention, children are merely victims of the teacher's whim. It is vital, therefore, that learning intentions should be shared with children in every lesson...

(Clarke 2001)

Shirley Clarke quite deliberately chooses to employ the term 'learning intentions' and not 'learning objectives' when referring to what should be taking place in lessons. 'Intention' suggests a much more specific target or goal, and the term demands greater specificity on the part of the teacher(s) devising these clear purposes.

Working with teachers on this matter during the last two years I have become convinced that, almost perversely, they need to work in a very narrow language framework, certainly in the first stages of development, if they are to make this aspect of their planning as powerful as it should be. Many primary teachers of literacy have already been through this stage of their development, and those who are familiar with this way of structuring their lessons have become very adept at constructing demanding and learning-focused intentions. Those primary teachers who have been impressed by the recommendations of Shirley Clarke have adopted the terms 'WALT' ('We Are Learning To') and 'WILF' ('What I Am Looking For' – used by the teacher to anticipate the outcomes of the learning) and 'TIB' ('This Is Because') in the early stages of their lessons, to help their pupils concentrate more certainly on what they should be aiming to achieve. These terms are probably too young for secondary school pupils to use comfortably (although teachers might find them helpful as a personal mental aide-memoire), which is why the term 'learning intention' is preferable.

Because – if we accept the advice of Bowring-Carr and West-Burnham (1997) – 'learning' means bringing about a wholesale intellectual change, and affects the ways that future thinking is formulated, the intentions pointing out what that learning is to be should be expressed in ways that ensure genuine cognitive impact. I therefore recommend to teachers that they do not use the language of the *Framework* documents, as discussed in Chapter 1 (p. 19). Words such as:

> to explore / identify / discover / bring about / review / recognise / appreciate / collect / investigate / experiment with / find and use / reflect on / trace the ways / experiment with / develop ideas / make good use of / develop and signpost etc.
>
> (all taken from the *Framework for Teaching English: Years 7, 8 and 9*, DfEE 2001a)

cannot, of themselves, bring about the sort of intellectual change necessary to qualify as real 'learning'. As a pupil, I might be given a learning intention: 'to *explore* the changes taking place in…'; or 'to *review* the ways that…'. I might then undertake considerable 'exploration' or 'review', but yet still have very little idea about what results or outcomes that 'exploration' or 'review' should lead to. I would have been assigned an *activity*, but nothing in that supposed learning intention has assisted me in being able to pinpoint what I should be *learning*. It is my contention that this sort of misunderstanding has been taking place for many years in English lessons (although, of course, not exclusively lessons in English). Pupils have regularly been given huge numbers of activities to undertake in their lessons – sometimes, extremely creative and demanding activities – yet what the pupils should, intellectually, have taken from those lessons that could contribute significantly to their future experiences, which would be capable of changing those pupils' approaches and expectations, which would have changed those pupils in important ways, has not been carefully considered or articulated for them. Such practices have led to what has sometimes popularly been termed 'a checklist curriculum', that is, teachers have covered huge areas of the intended curriculum with their classes, and can show that all the listed features have been visited by their classes, but they often feel hugely frustrated because the pupils seem not to have made anything like the progress that was expected. Many secondary teachers have complained about the new Key Stage 3 English Strategy because it seems to suggest a 'checklist' approach, without fully realising that they have to fashion the suggested content into more supportive learning programmes.

The smallest linguistic sleights of hand, however, can offer a very different way of framing what takes place in classrooms to set up a much clearer focus on the actual *learning* intended. This better attention can be brought about by using verbs that are related to cognitive processes, rather than the active processes described above. So the most powerful words from which to construct the most effective learning intentions are: **to know**, or **to understand**.

But to illustrate how to employ these ideas in real learning examples, I need to explore two sorts of learning, which I will term 'unit learning' and 'short-term learning'.

'Unit learning' and 'short-term learning'

Earlier in this chapter I suggested what the **characteristics of good learning and progress in English/literacy** might be, and stated that some of the most fundamental learning that pupils undertake would enable them to know such things as how to be, for example:

- clear about the purposes of texts, and understand how their forms and linguistic and meaning-making structures and devices fulfil those purposes; and

- able to relate texts to the contexts in which they were constructed.

These huge overview aspirations are what the totality of English/literacy lessons should be contributing towards; they represent the ultimate goal of all learning in the subject. As vital as they are, however, it would not be possible to keep offering them to every class for each lesson. They would be too remote for most pupils to make good use of and regard as supportive requisites, and would seem extremely boring and demotivating if constantly repeated. It is therefore necessary to stage the ways by which pupils come to these ends. The planning proforma (Figure 3.1) on page 60 sets out how this staging might be done; through identifying a 'Key learning intention' (the overall 'unit learning') for the whole unit of however many lessons, and the contributory 'learning intention' of

Key Learning Intention:

Year: **Class:** **Teacher:** **Resources:**

Objectives: **Word/sentence:**
   Reading:
   Writing:
   Speaking and listening:

	Word/sentence (10 mins)	Learning Intention	Introduction/focus of new teaching	Development/independent consolidation	Success Criteria	Plenary/Self Evaluation (10 mins)	Home-work
1.							
2.							
3.							
4.							

Speaking and Listening Opportunities:

Figure 3.1 Planning proforma

each lesson within that unit ('short-term learning'). In fact, it would be unrealistic to think of a separate learning intention for each lesson – and actual lessons rarely work in that neat manner! My recommendation would be for teachers to think of at least one learning intention, with perhaps one or two more, for up to three lessons. There could be more than one learning intention for one, two or three lessons. For instance, there could be a text-level, a sentence-level and, possibly, a word-level learning intention being undertaken simultaneously, but I would not encourage teachers to foreground more than one learning intention in each of those categories at a time. The most important aspect is not how many learning intentions are expected to be packed into the space of each lesson, but the quality and long-lasting effectiveness of each learning intention in the further learning in the subject – and whether, of course, they were truly learned.

So an English teacher might decide to select as an example of 'unit learning', for a series of 15 hour-long lessons, the following outline intention:

> To know that texts in…genre share particular characteristics, designed to have…effect on readers, which pupils will identify in their reading and demonstrate in their construction of texts…etc.

Whilst this intention would be shared regularly with the pupils throughout the duration of the unit – certainly, as an absolute minimum, once every lesson – it would need to be staged in smaller parts for one, two or three lessons at a time. Quite reasonably, the first few lessons might have the shorter-term learning intention, e.g. 'To know that texts in…genre share the following core characteristics', etc. While teachers are listing these necessary characteristics or features, they should also be considering what the 'success criteria' might be to 'prove' or demonstrate that this learning has, indeed, taken place. They should be identifying what sort of exercise or activity would be appropriate and sufficiently powerful to enable pupils to verify that they are confident and secure in the knowledge and understanding they have recently acquired. Such demonstrations, of course, are likely to be differentiated, to enable more able pupils to indicate their greater insights, while nevertheless allowing even the most hesitant learners to show that some genuine progress has been made.

The establishment of 'success criteria' should not be a mysterious, hidden process to which the pupils have no access. They should, as they become increasingly confident with these learning-focused procedures, be made partners in the agreement of 'success criteria', as proof that they understand what they are supposed to be pursuing by articulating what would be regarded as worthwhile outcomes of their study. I have seen Year 5 pupils in a primary school perfectly capable of devising their own 'success criteria' from the 'learning intention'. The teacher of the class always allocated a few minutes at the beginning of each lesson, after having discussed the 'learning intention', for the pupils to discuss the sorts of appropriate criteria to underscore that the learning had been successful. They shared the various suggestions from each group, and then decided which were the most taxing and challenging, before choosing what everybody would aim for.

David Perkins, in his book *Smart Schools*, makes an important case about 'understanding' as 'a multi-layered thing':

> not just to do with particulars but with our whole mindset about a discipline or subject matter...If a pedagogy of understanding means anything, it means understanding the piece in the context of the whole and the whole as the mosaic of its pieces.

(Perkins 1992)

He goes on to challenge teachers to recognise that:

> Knowing is a state of possession, and I can easily check whether learners possess the knowledge they are supposed to. But understanding somehow goes beyond possession. The person who understands is capable of 'going beyond the information given', in Jerome Bruner's eloquent phrase. To understand understanding, we have to get clearer about that 'beyond possession'.

(ibid.)

Perkins then offers suggestions of what learners ought to be able to do with their knowledge to demonstrate that they are not merely in a state of 'possession', but have moved on to 'enablement', by being able to: 'explain, exemplify, apply, justify, compare and contrast, contextualise or generalise' as a result of what they know. These are the sorts of verbs that could act as good guides for the establishment of valid and worthwhile 'success criteria' to bring about what we might ultimately think of as 'deep knowledge'.

Planning for long-term, medium-term and short-term learning

These areas of learning are the same. Their titles merely remind us of the scale of learning and the order of learning planning so that we can shape the most supportive, sensible and coherently staged curriculum for our pupils during the period of their secondary schooling.

To begin the process of planning for strong learning, the team of English staff will need to have agreed a set of agreed outcomes, as suggested on page 55. Without this necessary 'map' it will not be possible to plot the separate themes or threads across the five years in Key Stages 3 and 4, that will be working cumulatively to achieve the sorts of outcomes the department is intending. So *long-term planning* is an essential prerequisite, to set up a shared and clearly articulated sense of the overall learning that will have been achieved by the department for all pupils by end of Year 11. It would mean the agreement of 'threads' of progress possible to trace through each of the secondary years, e.g.:

All pupils will have learned the following in their English lessons during the five years they study in this school:

- – all readers are potential writers;
- – all texts are purposeful and are written for specifically imagined audiences; and
- – the meanings of texts are related to their form and structure etc.

Readers will realise that these sorts of statements are derived directly from the 'characteristics of good learning and progress in English and literacy' defined on pages 55 and 56, which would be the starting point for this overview.

English teachers should decide and set out the span of textual experiences they anticipate for their pupils across the five years of Key Stages 3 and 4, and then break the learning associated with each of those textual encounters into stages. So all departments will have to study poetry, because the National Curriculum instructs them to, the GCSE examination expects them to and most English teachers will want to. Effective *long-term planning* of poetry, however, will only be truly possible, if the teachers have articulated a clear idea of what they want their pupils to *learn* about poetry, and then to stage that learning year on year. As a simple example, if the department wants pupils to recognise that one of the essential features to be learned about poetry is that 'the meaning in poetry is conveyed through a combination of particular stylistic effects – such as rhyme, rhythm, metre etc.' – what would the stages of progression in learning be associated with these features across the five-year programme? Such cumulative approaches would enable teachers of Year 11 classes to be far more assured that their pupils have a solid foundation on which to build their current learning, and those students would not be approaching the poets in their examination anthology in isolation, but would be capable of recognising more readily the relationships between them. There will be very few English departments that have already established a clear overview of the learning to be pursued and planned for with regard to poetry – or for other sorts of textual material.

One practical exercise that a department could usefully undertake would be to count up the possible number of hours that any one pupil would be exposed to study English during their time in the school. Given that most pupils in Key Stage 3 have a timetable that includes something like three one-hour periods of English a week, that means a maximum number of hours of specific English study will be three (number of years) times three (periods each week) times 39 (number of weeks the school is in session) = 359. Two more years of the same allocation in Key Stage 4 would add 234 hours. So the overall time that any pupil could study in school under teacher supervision would amount to 593 hours. That total assumes that every period would be dedicated to study; in reality, there will be numerous other distractions. Tests, examinations, mock exams, feedback time, school events, and the other genuine distractions of school life will soon erode that available time to somewhere much nearer 500 hours. That means no more than the equivalent of 20 full school weeks (at 25 hours a week) in which to provide a whole English programme. When considered against the possible range of texts available in the world with a potential for study, and the potential learning from them, 500 hours is really not a very long time at all. Which makes the imperative for deciding *exactly* what will be studied, and what the core *overall learning goals* must be even more vital, if the pupils are to be given the very best opportunities.

Medium-term planning should then track each of the separate identified 'threads' of learning through every one of the year programmes, to ensure that each appears in the planning and that the stages of their development are genuinely progressive. I often observe poetry lessons in Year 9 that fail to develop what has been important in lessons taught in Years 7 and 8. They have often been the sorts of lessons that Shirley Clarke describes as 'contexts'; introspective and free-standing, rather than staged developments on the way to the acquisition of ultimate learning goals. Rather than focusing attention simply on poetry, regarding poetry as a special, self-supporting area of study, it is vital to see what relationship poetry does and does not have with other textual materials. Why do poets choose poetry as their medium of textual interaction? What are the possibilities poetry opens up to the poet that are not available, for instance, to the novelist? What is 'poetic prose'? Why might a poet choose to write in the sonnet form? What would be its benefits and constraints? What relationship does the balladeer have with the teller of prose traditional tales?

'Medium term' could mean different ways of organising learning for different departments. Having established the full overview of total English/language/literacy/literary learning as the 'long term', departments could then either divide that learning package into yearly sub-packages, or divide the learning into key stage units. So, for instance, a department identifying 'narrative' as an important area of textual learning they would wish to develop through the school might decide to teach and revisit 'narrative' every year, or alternatively they might ensure that a large unit of 'narrative' textual study would appear once, at some stage in Key Stage 3, and a more challenging and progressive unit would also be planned for Key Stage 4. So the pupils might encounter five smaller units of 'narrative' related work, or two large study units. Such decisions would depend, to some extent, on the learning capabilities of the pupils. The practices of 'packaging' learning might change from five annual units to two much more comprehensive modules as pupils are encouraged to change their attitudes to learning.

Medium-term plans would be able to indicate at which point of the course the different identified strands of learning should appear for each of the secondary year groups. Planned thoughtfully, they will enable teachers to anticipate the work demands made on pupils, and the assessment procedures to be carried out. They should also serve as useful indicators of where various resources will be required, the specialist rooms and support that might be needed, and possible trips and prospective visiting guests might be booked. Effective and mature medium-term planning can be extremely valuable to teachers when undertaken in these ways as it is capable of making teachers' workloads more straightforward and less demanding and stressful.

Short-term planning (or unit planning)

Most departments plan their work in each year group around units of work, intended to cohere different areas of textual study, usually incorporating pupils working in what George Keith, the linguist, calls 'the four gerunds of English': reading, writing, speaking and listening. Historically, a considerable amount of that planning has been built on what Shirley Clarke (see p. 54) has described as the 'context' of the learning, rather than in the substantial learning intention itself:

> There is still a need to sort out learning intentions at the planning stage. Too many learning intentions are in fact activities and contain the context of the learning. Deciding success criteria for muddled learning intentions, focusing the lesson and subsequent feedback is problematic. It doesn't help that many of the QCA SoW learning objectives are muddled in this way. When learning intentions are 'pure', context free, the success criteria work like a dream, the lesson focuses appropriately and the feedback is obvious. Most importantly, the connections are made clear for the children; the learning intention can apply to a number of contexts.
>
> (Clarke 2003a)

Typically, a group of English teachers will include units of work for each year group based on such textual material as a class novel (or two), a non-fiction text, some poetry study, a play (often by Shakespeare), something to do with changing language, a media text, some ICT-generated writing and, perhaps, a specifically focused speaking module. Given that a school year is a maximum of 39 weeks, and there are eight separate areas outlined above, each unit could, at best, expect to have four weeks assigned to its study, a maximum of probably no more than 12 lessons in most schools. Concentrating on learning in such circumstances is utterly paramount; otherwise pupils encounter a series of experiences over a relatively short period that may not add up to a great deal of collective value, however fascinating the separate experiences might have been.

Short-term planning cannot exist successfully in its own right. If the long-term overview of what the teachers are collaboratively aiming to achieve with the majority of pupils has not been agreed, then short-term planning will not be clearly centred and will lack real purpose. The coherence and main aims of the department's work have to be in place long before the contents and intended outcomes of actual lessons are written. If, however, an English team has such guiding documentation already published, then the plans for each unit or module are much more easily constructed, and are capable of straightforward review and possible amendment.

The example of short-term planning illustrated on page 60 offers a possible new direction for English departments. The illustrated page shows spaces for only four days of planning, but on a simple computer program, spaces for any number of lessons could be published. Most units or modules of work in secondary schools take place over four or five weeks, usually, the equivalent of 12–15 hours of classroom time. This form of planning has a number of advantages. The first important reminder is the 'Key Learning Intention' at the top of the page. Teachers have to ask themselves 'What will the pupils take from this module that has changed the way they now think about what comprises the focus of the study; what will they now be able to do (or think or use) that they were not able to deploy previously, and how will their future learning be supported by what has been acquired in this study?'

No longer, if such approaches to planning were made, would teachers think in terms of 'a poetry module', 'a prose fiction module' or even a 'Macbeth' module. Instead they would be focusing their own and their pupils' energies and attention on more tangible and assessable factors. So, the 'Year 8 poetry' module might have 'key learning intentions' expressed as 'to understand that poets use imagery in particular ways to make their meanings'. The 'prose fiction module' could be 'to know the principal features of science fiction novels'; the 'Macbeth module' might be 'to know how Shakespeare uses dramatic verse to create a sense of evil'.

All of these suggestions are deliberately problematic, and might not be the focus adopted by considerable numbers of teachers in respect of each of the illustrated forms of text. But that is very much my point. English teachers will have a massive range of starting points, or areas of main focus in regard to all this material. Of course, there could be more than one 'Key Learning Intention' for each module – although too many would diminish the notion of 'key'.

The members of a department should sit down together and come to some sort of agreement about what they believe are the central concerns possible to be studied and understood by the pupils they work with daily, from the materials they are employing, and that conform to the overall learning intentions of that group. Such discussions ought to be difficult and searching. But they will contribute hugely to the ongoing development of learning at the centre of the department's work. I want to make it absolutely clear that I do not want to restrict the pupils' learning through this approach – if other learning transpires or is brought about, then that extra provision must be seen as a genuine bonus to be noted and celebrated. There is nothing mechanistic, one-dimensional or otherwise restrictive about what has been proposed above. This way of thinking about what should be taking place in lessons substantially supports the least confident pupils, and offers secure learning starting points for those who are more capable.

A department I have been working with came up with the following core learning intentions for the modules they chose to include in their Key Stage 3 programme. They still found it helpful to have a title for each module, and I offer their first suggestions, not as exemplar material, but as illustrations of a group of teachers developing a learning vocabulary that was new to them:

Title	Learning Intention
A study of different poetic forms and techniques linked by a theme	• To understand how different poets use structural and linguistic features in a selection of poems to add to the effect and appreciation of the subject matter. • To know how to select important common features in poems and to compare them effectively.
How non-fiction and media texts can manipulate the 'reader'	• To understand that non-fiction and media texts can have a variety of purposes. • To know the characteristics of persuasive texts through studying examples and constructing appropriate texts.

These teachers are talking together differently as a result of beginning to think in a new way about their shared work. 'To understand that non-fiction and media texts can have a variety of purposes' is still not as developed as it could be, but this intention is much more firmly focused than the headings previously employed by this department.

Having come to such agreement, it should be possible for the teachers to move more quickly to the suggested outcomes of the module. They can expect, perhaps, some written work capable of demonstrating unequivocally that the bulk of the year group, or individual class, has understood the nature of the work being studied, and is in a position to use that knowledge in a range of ways – as David Perkins outlined on page 62. The teachers might, on the other hand, set up a drama presentation, or a multimedia (or at least mixed-media) final portfolio, or a round of pupil presentations. The actual outcome is entirely in the command of the teachers concerned, as long as the criteria of pupils displaying that they have genuinely learned has been met. The other feature to highlight about such to planning the short-term unit is that the teachers can, of course, ever relevant texts they choose in order to reach the conclusion being above. They do *not* need to employ the same texts as other colleagues not wish to do so. As long as the learning goals are understood by every teac... and are being assiduously pursued in each classroom, the textual resources are entirely at the discretion of each teacher in the department (departmental resources allowing).

Establishing these 'key learning intentions' at the time of drawing up the medium-term plans is actually a good idea for everybody concerned. By so doing, the department will be able to ascertain the range of learning possibilities anticipated over the span of a taught school year, and can, at a suitable distance, make any necessary adjustments to ensure good acknowledgement of breadth and balance of the curriculum. The teachers can also give themselves good notice of the range of resources they will require to make available to support the identified learning – and perhaps make unusual or unexpected combinations of textual materials to stir new insights and stimulate pupil interest in ways not possible in the past.

The first column on the planning example shown on page 60 is entirely optional. It was added by members of my Literacy Team in the early days of introducing this planning model, when we were encouraging teachers to begin their lessons with active, lively, stimulating 'starter activities' that would immediately engage the pupils' interest and set up expectations for the rest of the lesson. The reality has been different in a number of schools! Advisory colleagues, who continue to work regularly in secondary classrooms, often share with me their perceptions that they have never seen so much decontextualised work taking place in English, and that a large portion of the blame lies with the introduction of the 'starter', whose purpose has not been properly understood by some departments and individual teachers. I would not want the planning sheet as a whole to be rejected because one part of it did not meet with approval by a few departments.

There are two really important columns on the main body of the planning sheet; the one headed 'Learning intention' and the one headed, 'Success criteria'. These are the main business of the page, relating directly with the 'Key Learning Intention', and they should be discussed and dealt with together. The Learning Intention applies to what is expected to be learned in the lesson. In fairness, it is about what would be expected to be learned in up to three lessons, as it really is not realistically possible, or desirable, to parcel out a bit of learning for every lesson, as I explained earlier. Learning in English regularly requires a good deal of 'immersion' in text, and some exploration and finding out before real learning security can be established.

So it is reasonable to think of a learning topic taking place over one, two or three lessons, but this learning topic would feed into the overall Key Learning Intention for the whole unit. An example might be an overall Key Learning

Intention, such as the following: 'Pupils will understand how persuasion texts achieve their goals, and construct successful persuasion texts of their own, in different media'. The first few lessons of such a unit would require the pupils to have a good understanding of the features that characterise 'persuasion' texts. Therefore, the first three lessons might share a Learning Intention: 'to know the characteristics of persuasive texts'. The pupils would be exposed to a range of persuasive texts, in different media, conducting exploratory analysis, to identify the features they share in common.

The 'success criteria' might then be applied at the conclusion of the third lesson, when pupils might be asked to consider another example of a persuasion text, new to them, and be expected to recognise the characteristics that it shares with others in the genre. Or a group might be asked to make a presentation about what they have discovered – or, if time and resources allow, to make a text containing the agreed features. Teachers would then be in a position to decide how much learning had taken place and how well their teaching was being understood, *and* what adjustments they might need to carry out to ensure that the largest proportion of the class was making progress in this area. Well-structured plenary sessions (not always necessarily taking place at the end of lessons, but properly used as summaries wherever they are employed) would allow pupils some self-reflection time to consider what might have been learned.

Teachers should try to encourage their pupils to suggest worthwhile 'success criteria' to demonstrate that genuine learning has taken place. I have seen pupils in primary schools successfully challenged to offer their own substantial success criteria, and it should be possible for secondary pupils to grow in this respect. Knowing what is expected as evidence of learning is a really valuable way of making it clear that the learning intentions have been fully understood, and that they are helping the pupils focus on what has been identified as the most important aspects of the module.

The Year 5 teacher I quoted on page 39, who is very confident with planning in this manner, addresses her class on large pieces of paper, displayed at the front of the room, in the following manner:

> By the ..., you will know that there are different ways to open a story by showing me two different story openings that you have written.

> You will also know that characters can be presented through different aspects of narration, including word choice. You will show me this by writing a new character or episode into a story, employing one of the aspects we have studied.

Or:

> By..., you will understand the dramatic conventions of plays, by performing a scene from a play you have written, that includes the conventions we have studied.

Secondary teachers are likely to want to make the language a little more appropriate for their pupils, but they would find it difficult to be any clearer in the way they convey success criteria related to learning intentions. The assessment focus for the pupils' understanding is also very apparent in such an approach.

This 'column' of the planning page could also be an excellent opportunity for a teacher to differentiate the expectations being made on a class. The success criteria of all pupils need not be the same, although they could be involved in much the same work. A few might be required to produce a range of evidence from the lesson, to demonstrate that learning has taken place in ways commensurate with the potential of individuals or groups.

Focusing on learning in this manner brings about a number of benefits. Teachers have to think carefully about what significant matter they want their pupils to take from these lessons, to be referred to and employed in related and other contexts, and how that learning can be constructed in supportive stages. Teachers are readier to express very clearly to their pupils what they wish them to concentrate on. Pupils are in no doubt about what the centre of their learning should be, which can be extremely helpful for less able pupils, but just as helpful for those with more linguistic confidence. As I have mentioned already, if other learning, not included on the planning sheet, takes place, then teachers should be pleased and ready to acknowledge this 'bonus'. But the really essential issue of shared and understood learning outcomes being articulated, pursued and achieved will have been more fully addressed.

The other sections of the planning sheet enable the teacher to outline the sorts of activities they might be setting up, the groupings in which the pupils will be placed, and any other relevant details that they believe are necessary to include. The relative sizes of the various boxes are a matter of personal, or collective departmental, taste – they are not fixed, but easily moved. Teachers I know, who regularly use this form of planning, write all over the sheet after it has been originally composed, either evaluating lessons, and writing recommendations to themselves, or merely reminding themselves about specific issues they might wish to raise or questions they want to be certain to put. The real point about the sheet is that it should be utterly flexible, serve as a plan and as ongoing record, and contribute to the assessment that follows from the lessons it outlines. Notable achievement, or instances of underachievement, are recorded by some teachers on the back of their planning forms. These notes act as records, to remind teachers either to raise their expectations for a few pupils, or to ensure that certain learning features are repeated for those still not fully understanding what the real centre of the learning is about.

Explanatory note

Much of the rest of the book will be about exploring what substantial learning might look like, and the sorts of foundations on which it can be properly established, through the areas of reading, writing, and speaking and listening. Ever since the publication of the HMI document *English 5–16 – Curriculum Matters* (DES 1984) enshrined study in English in these 'four gerunds', it has been usual to categorise what takes place in planning and assessment terms under those headings. Yet, the fullest definition of 'reading' has shifted considerably in the 20 years since that document, and 'reading' no longer merely applies to the making of meaning in print. Similarly, 'writing' is, 20 years on, imbued with far more text construction possibility for pupils than would have been regarded a natural part of school experience in the mid-1980s. The digitalisation of various technologies has meant that it is possible for still cameras, video cameras, DVD players, microphones and computers to 'talk to each other' in different permutations to bring about texts containing still and moving images, and sound and written text in all sorts of styles – all within the grasp of quite small children.

But reading, writing, speaking and listening are not the only ways in which study in the subject might be categorised. It would, for instance, be equally feasible to set up study, particularly in our times, about general textual awareness and understanding, in which the generic features of texts – whether written, read, spoken or listened to, and the overlaps of those forms – were the focused areas of studies. The 'multimodal' approach to textual study, being investigated in the work of Gunther Kress (2003), Elaine Millard (2003) and Eve Bearne (2003), offers new starting points for a whole range of different intellectual relationships sparked off between many sorts of texts, from a number of possible different directions.

Equally powerful might be arguments about the need to outline courses that embrace knowing and reflecting on what it means to be 'literate' in a modern and constantly changing society, in which most of the possible developments of the future can only be glimpsed and briefly sketched.

> What it means to be literate as an adult in late twentieth-century Britain is thus much harder to define. Where once the tensions in defining literacy revolved around the differences between minimal measures (the ability to sign a name) and what might count as full literacy... now there is a question as to whether literacy can still be seen as a singular concept. There is also the question whether, within the multiple literacies that might replace the notion of an autonomous and culture-free literacy... it is also necessary to extend the term to include the ways in which we read a range of situations and media. It is increasingly difficult to separate written and spoken English in many textual contexts. Bookshops and libraries reflect this change, offering not just books, but also magazines, audiotapes, CD-ROMs, music, and introducing live performances, evening openings and coffee shops.
>
> (Robinson 2000)

Nevertheless, whatever visionary possibilities *ought* to qualify as the essential content of 'English' studies in schools in the future, the reality is likely to be much more routine. Any government facing curriculum change and possible review in English would still find itself having to satisfy a hugely diverse range of different interest groups – from, at one end, readers of the *Daily Mail*, who would regard any tampering with the already very shaky (as they understand it) *status quo* as the final straw in any battle to maintain standards, to those university researchers and teachers, and many advisers, who believe that school-based English is currently situated in the equivalent of the 'dark ages'. Any reform, however necessary, is not going to challenge the current boundaries of the subject, and any changes will probably remain firmly within those recognisable boundaries already defining the subject, fuzzy though they may be. Therefore, while I would enjoy the indulgence of investigating alternative approaches, such considerations would probably not be fruitful in the context of this book.

> Central to the myth of English as a school subject is the notion of tradition, and in particular of a long history of an unchanging and unchallenged approach to English in schools and universities. Alongside this goes an everyday view of the content of the subject which ignores the tensions between literacy and literature and between reception and production.
>
> (Robinson 2000)

Whatever the scope of any changes that will emerge during the next few years, teachers will still have massive responsibilities to ensure that the evolving linguistic needs of their pupils are being properly identified and wholly met; which is why, in the following chapters, I have chosen to work within familiar subject territorial boundaries.

Improving learning in reading

Lord of the Flies; *Kes*; *Of Mice and Men*; *An Inspector Calls*; *Animal Farm*; *Across the Barricades*; *Talking in Whispers* and many of the other texts that have figured in secondary English have never existed officially within the borders of English Literature. These texts have been brought together by no recognized procedure at all. No-one has ever attempted to justify the existence of this secondary canon. There is no common agreement on what texts exactly are to be included in it or where its limits might be drawn. No-one has ever determined why these texts are peculiarly suited to the study of English at this level. Why they are there remains a mystery; their official status remains unjustified. They represent the practice of a subject that is – in a philosophical sense – ungrounded.

(Peim 1993)

Learning in reading, and learning about reading are topics that I have not seen explored in much detail – particularly in the secondary educational sector – during my own English teaching and advisory career of over thirty years. In a book I published about reading in secondary schools, first published in 2000, I made the following claim:

Reading is not taught in most secondary schools in England. Considerable numbers of activities in connection with books and other sorts of texts take place in classrooms, but these are not usually directed towards the improvement and growth of pupils' reading, except in a very limited sense.

(Dean 2000/2003)

If, as I still assert, the direct teaching of reading (and the robust assessment systems that ought to underpin such teaching) has not developed substantially since that claim was first made – despite the best efforts of those responsible for the English strand of the Key Stage 3 Strategy – then the amount of planned learning resulting from that level of teaching will not be considerable. Many pupils will have acquired the wherewithal to undertake focused activities related to texts, but they will not, as a general rule, have learned a great deal about the overall meaning-making issues of reading.

This book will spend more time exploring the learning of reading than the learning involved in the other areas of English, because I have become increasingly convinced during a professional lifetime in the subject that if pupils are not willing, comfortable and critically aware readers, then everything else in children's literacy development is delayed until those qualities have begun to be established and recognised.

reading is seen to be the foundational capability in the acquisition of literacy

(Andrews 2001)

reading not only increases our life skills and extends our knowledge, it goes much deeper – I want to argue that in many respects reading determines how we are able to think, that it has a fundamental effect on the development of the imagination, and thus exerts a powerful influence on the development of the emotional and moral as well as verbal intelligence and therefore on the kind of person we are capable of becoming.

(Harrison 2004)

As vital as good writing skills are (and we should remember that writing is so disproportionately privileged in all the formal assessment procedures adopted through the whole educational system – even reading is usually assessed through writing!), some aspect of reading is usually serving most people most of their waking lives; while that situation is nothing like as true for writing. Most adults need really good reasons to undertake any sort of writing: reading – for the literate – is inescapable. Therefore, a well-formulated sense of what reading is actually about should be the foundation of a reliable and sound English programme. Peter Traves goes further:

The overarching aim of schools ought to be the production of confident, ambitious and critical readers who see reading, like other aspects of their language facility, as a key part in their engagement in and understanding of the world.

(Traves 1994)

Part of the problem about the teaching and learning of reading in the modern English classroom can be seen in the commonly held attitude typified by Michael Fleming and David Stevens in their admirable book *English Teaching in the Secondary School*, where they conclude a chapter on reading in the following manner:

In the final analysis the way to achieve progress in reading is to build on enthusiasm – not only for the pleasure of imaginative (generally fiction) reading, but for unlocking the secrets of text because one wants to find out what is there. In the reality of the classroom this means suggesting more demanding, stimulating texts to be read in more sophisticated ways…After all, we tend to forget that reading is meant to be for pleasure.

(Fleming and Stevens 1998)

That last statement really must be challenged, although to do so invites the danger of being regarded as a heretic, beyond the pale of mainstream English, by some teachers of the subject. I would like to suggest that reading is not 'meant to be for pleasure', and if it is, teachers of reading have then been consigned a nearly impossible task, always likely to result in the worst sorts of frustration. Reading is much broader in scope and involves rather more important interactions than the suggestion made above:

> When we speak about reading we usually have in mind the reading of a particular kind of text – one that is in the form of printed language. Sometimes the assumption is even more specific, referring only to books or even to particular kinds of books termed literature. In general parlance we use the verb 'to read' much more widely. We talk, for example, of reading faces, tea leaves, the weather, people. There is a common expression, 'I can read you like a book'. This broader definition is highly significant. It is indicative of the fact that the reading of print is only one instance of a much more widely applied human faculty. Paulo Freire and Donaldo Macedo subtitled their book on literacy *Reading the Word and the World*. That is what we all do; we read the world around us. We give meaning to the patterns we see in it. We are active makers of meaning: we read meaning out of and into the world. Each of us reads our own unique version of that meaning but we do so within the constraints and conventions of the cultural networks in which we live our lives.
>
> (Traves 1994)

The differences expressed by these two approaches matter very much, and are extremely relevant to the sorts of issues being explored by this book. If reading is just about 'pleasure', teachers' work would be much more superficially based and more focused. Lessons could be occupied with seeking what pupils enjoyed most, and considerable time could then be spent indulging in and heightening the pleasures the identified texts offered. Examination and assessment would also be effortless: 'Name your favourite text and explain the pleasure it gives you'! In the early years of the twenty-first century, a number of popular writers of books for children, including Philip Pullman, David Almond and Michael Morpurgo, have lamented that the sort of study of texts promoted by the Literacy Strategies in primary schools and Key Stage 3 fails to contribute to the 'pleasure' of reading, and there has been neglect of the word 'enjoy' in all related documentation. They are reflecting an attitude that has traditionally been dominant for too long in English teaching in secondary schools; one that requires re-balancing if better learning about reading is to be achieved – but which does not necessarily mean that 'pleasure', 'enjoyment' and 'delight' will be diminished in any way. They should – properly addressed within a much more mature programme of learning to read – actually be enhanced.

In making this case, I would like to make it perfectly clear that I really do believe that all readers should experience pleasure in their reading. I regard reading fiction as one of my most passionately loved and enjoyable pastimes. I genuinely want to encourage an atmosphere and ethos in which enjoyment in reading is one of the desirable outcomes of all the textual study taking place in schools and elsewhere. There is so much to be enjoyed in certain sorts of reading, especially, but certainly not exclusively, in works of fiction for huge numbers of readers. There are many different personal pleasures to be discovered and tasted, and learning is surely made more likely where the learners are experiencing positive feelings about the matters in which they are involved. There is also, however, more than a suggestion in the quotation from Fleming and Stevens that the sort of reading being emphasised is heavily biased in favour of involvement with fiction texts. Such an inclination has been true of English teachers generally, who have overwhelmingly chosen fictional material as the focus of classroom attention, in some respects further reducing their claim to be regarded as 'teachers of reading'.

Peter Traves reminds us of the enormity of the demands of reading for all of us:

> In defining the nature of reading and readers we must consider the role reading plays in our society. We live in a society that assumes print literacy (it also increasingly assumes other forms of media literacy such as computer and television literacy). Every day demands are placed on us as readers of print. We read at work, as we drive, as we shop. There are few aspects of our lives that are not linked in one way or another to the reading of print. The institutions of our economy, our government and our culture rest upon written language and depend upon the capacity to read...Reading plays a particularly important role in education. Not only does our education system demand a lot of reading in the process of learning, it also tends to use the capacity to read fluently as an indicator of more general intellectual ability.
>
> (Traves 1994)

He also acknowledges that 'Reading is a major source of pleasure in our society'. His broad and extensive sweep across the areas of our lives in which competent reading abilities are so necessary should remind us of the massive scale the most supportive reading curriculum ought to be.

Recent research and insight into the processes of reading have begun to indicate just how much a rethinking of the topic is required by those who have a professional interest in the promotion and greater development of reading. Those who previously knew little about the subject will be strongly challenged by the extent of new considerations they will have to face if they are to make any real headway. Listening to a lecturer in teacher education, as I did in April 2004, outline her department's PGCE programme for potential secondary teachers of English, all expected to take place in 28 days of tutoring, it was not difficult to realise that very scant time is available to teach them much about any aspect of the subject, let alone reading.

Any approach I take towards reading can, of course, only be partial, otherwise this book would be wholly devoted to the learning of reading. But it is worth realising, in passing, the extent of the knowledge the fullest textual meaning-making procedures are expecting each of us to activate if we are to be thought of as properly 'reading' in the multimodal contextual settings in which we all exist. Eve Bearne, in a powerful article about 'rethinking literacy' in our times, writes:

> The affordance of a text is bound up with the ways in which it is constructed. Writing in a book affords different possibilities compared with broadcasting on television. Different types of text have varying patterns of cohesion depending what the text affords to the reader or viewer. Those who are represented through written narrative or report depend on chronological cohesion. Those which are represented visually or diagrammatically depend on spatial cohesion. Texts relayed through the medium of sound (of a single voice) also depend on chronological logic, but in addition are made cohesive by repetitions, which would be redundant in written texts. Texts which are relayed and taken in through mimesis – plays, ballet, opera – combine both spatial and sound-repetitive cohesive devices, but in this case the spatial is three-dimensional. This relationship between affordances and material construction offered by the different modes and media influence the ways the texts are used, returned to, re-viewed or re-read. For example, whilst you can browse through a printed magazine, turning and returning the pages, you cannot (easily) do that with a radio or television magazine programme and certainly not a ballet.

> (Bearne 2003)

These are not the matters currently being addressed and tested through the prescribed National Curriculum.

This is not the place to determine what the contents of each school's reading curriculum should be (see the discussion on pages 83–85). Those particular and contextually dependent decisions should be the responsibility of individual departments, in collaboration with the other subject teachers in the school, paying regard to the requirements of the National Curriculum, and meeting the identified needs of their own pupils. In this section I want to explore the bigger issues of what it means to be a 'reader', what 'learning in reading' is about and why it is so utterly essential to underpin any decisions with solid theoretical and research-based knowledge.

What is meant by 'being a reader'

I regularly lead courses for secondary teachers of English where I ask the simple question: 'Who has ever been trained to teach reading?' At most, one or two teachers raise their hands hesitantly – and they are often former primary-trained teachers who have moved to secondary education, or have been 'special needs' teachers at some point in their careers. The usual answer is that nobody has been provided with more than the barest outline of reading training, for the reasons I suggested on page 76.

> Secondary school teachers of English in Britain have, traditionally, little experience in the teaching of reading which, in our training institutions, has been the purview of educational psychologists and primary school teachers. A great deal of research has passed unnoticed by those who could profit from it.
>
> (Meek, in Brindley 1994)

English teachers love reading. They talk readily and at length of the enormous pleasures they have experienced personally through a whole range of, usually, fiction books. They share their favourite titles with each other, and with anybody else willing to listen. They know how 'being carried away by reading' can offer some of the deepest and most moving experiences available to humans. They understand all too well how reading can 'transport' good readers, and the power it has to provide substantial vicarious experiences well beyond the ordinary lives of most readers. Andy Goodwyn has confirmed these reactions in his recent research:

> But there is a deep affinity with 'real' texts whether they be 'classic' or 'popular'. The sharing of such texts is where personal growth and the study of literature [mostly small 'l'] come together. The use of individual words can sometimes' reveal some powerful generalities. The word that I most frequently encounter in my conversations with English teachers over the years is 'love'. 'Love' is all you need, or, at least, a love of books, plays, poems, of the life of the imagination. English teachers are always telling me that they 'love' reading, and that they wish to convey this love to their students.
>
> (Goodwyn 2004)

Unfortunately, this is a form of love that can often be blind. English lessons are seen by many (and I include myself, when practising as a secondary English teacher, in this huge throng) as the opportunity to try to induct new young potential readers into the freemasonry of reading of a certain sort. This is a worthy and wholly respectable aim, but it is not, in the long run, actually about *teaching* reading; it is an approach shot through with all sorts of potential problems which do not, ultimately, significantly contribute to overall reading growth and development – what we might properly regard as 'learning'.

> Virtually all those involved in schooling – teachers, students and inspectors – had become disturbed about the lack of continuity in the reading experiences on offer at secondary level. Teachers expressed alarm at the apparent failures in cross-phase understanding and in comparing reading experiences at different ages. The majority of students at every stage up to university said they felt unprepared for the different reading demands facing them (Protherough 1989). This was also a recurrent note in the HMI report of summer 1989, concluding that practice was 'not underpinned by

sufficiently clear, coherent and comprehensive reading policies or organisation' (HMI 1989).

(Protherough 1995)

To move towards a position where 'learning' is being fully addressed, it is essential for the teachers involved to have gone through the processes of defining and agreeing what being a 'reader' might entail.

What is a reader?

For some years I have been encouraging colleagues to discuss in their departments those core characteristics or qualities they collectively believe would constitute a 'reader'. Put another way, which important indicators would identify the ideal 'reader' at the end of a programme of teaching reading in your school? Schools need to have clear views of these characteristics, to ensure that they are being planned and pursued in the teaching, can be understood by the pupils (who, after all, need to know what improvements they should be making), and tracked through an assessment system that is attuned to these features. Over time, I have worked with primary and secondary colleagues, read carefully through research findings and attended meetings focused on exploring the many 'strands' of reading. The following list is a synthesis of the matters that were covered in those events, possible to use at any stage of education. They are just as relevant for an A-level student of physics as they are for beginning readers in an Early Years class. They are valid for all forms of reading, whether of fiction or non-fiction, in printed form or other media. Each of these principles or qualities is capable of being divided into progressive stages or steps. They are all possible to improve, but no learner could ever conquer any of them. There will always be something new to achieve, and continuing life and literacy experiences means that every reader will discover more about reading than would previously have been planned for or anticipated before such extra occurrences took place.

The qualities or characteristics of the 'reader' I am recommending are (with a simple explanation of each in brackets):

1. A reader knows that reading is a complex, intellectual endeavour, requiring the reader to draw on a range of meaning-making skills.
   (Before worthwhile reading engagements can begin, the reader has to be aware that some sort of meaning will be sought – 'the brain has to be put in gear!')
2. A reader knows how to deploy previous knowledge of other texts to enable the effective meaning-making of the most recent textual encounter.
   (All reading is intertextual – it depends on relating experiences from other texts and the experiences from our lives to all new textual engagements.)

3. A reader knows that texts are constructed for clear purposes, for identifiable audiences and within recognisable text-types or genres.

(ALL texts are purposeful and created for identifiable reasons, and known audiences. Their purposes are closely reflected in their structures and language.)

4. A reader knows how to predict the way a text is likely to work, or be constructed, and can use that knowledge to confirm or re-adjust those predictions, depending on how typically the text proceeds.

(Being able to predict the ways texts are likely to proceed, or knowing that they contain predictable characteristics, greatly assists the process of meaning-making.)

5. A reader knows how to be critically active before encountering the substantial body of any text.

(Good readers are already asking questions of the text before engaging with the main content.)

6. A reader knows how to activate a growing repertoire of critical questions in engagements with new and unfamiliar texts.

(It is essential to be able to know which are the most appropriate and incisive questions to apply to unfamiliar textual materials to enable the quickest and most effective making of meaning and supportive intellectual engagement.)

7. A reader knows how to interact appropriately with a variety of text-types and genres.

(Different texts are read in different ways, and we do different things as a consequence of that reading. Knowing how to respond with regard to each sort of text is an important skill.)

8. A reader knows that an important way of demonstrating reading progression is through raising more complex questions about the same text.

(Getting better at reading is not about moving from simple to 'harder' texts; progression is gauged by the increasing range of tactics, skills and developing attitudes being applied to textual meaning-making.)

9. A reader knows that learning to read is a life-long process.

(No reader can ever be familiar with the whole available range of texts, and new sorts of texts are being constructed all the time. Being able to be flexible and exploratory in response is essential.)

10. A reader knows that other readers do not read and make meanings in the same ways.

(Every person brings unique life experiences and literary biographies to their reading; meaning is dependent on those experiences and engagements.)

11. A reader knows why a text might not satisfy its original requirements, or why a text has been rejected, unfinished.

(Knowing why texts have been chosen, and practising the making of effective choices, is a vital reading skill. Some texts do not fulfil their initial promise. Explaining why they fall short is another secure indicator of reading maturity.)

12. A reader knows that reading improves through self-monitoring of, and reflection on, own ability and progress.

(The more a reader understands about and considers their own reading strategies and tactics, and to what purposes reading is being put, the more that reader will recognise his/her own strengths and those aspects of his/her reading likely to benefit from improvement.)

Every one of these characteristics is very deliberately prefaced by the clause 'a reader knows', to stress their cognitive nature. If all readers are expected to 'know' these features of 'being a reader', then each feature is capable of being taught and assessed. Each separate strand embodies a long, progressive continuum of learning; it is never possible to be so highly proficient in any one of the strands that no further learning can be attempted. It is for teachers to have some sense of the present attainment of their pupils in respect of any one of these strands, and then to devise a programme of reading capable of promoting further growth and development along that strand.

In fact, the list above, whilst having the virtue of covering a broad sweep of 'reading', is far too large for any single department or school to manage or cover successfully. It requires careful and considered pruning, to agree priorities. Concentrating on about six strands or characteristics should be quite demanding enough for any group of staff; but such a focus could potentially lead to tangible reading growth for large numbers of pupils. I would like to suggest that the first and last listed 'quality', respectively emphasising, on the one hand, *intellectual engagement* and, at the other end of the scale, *reflection*, are non-negotiable. They are essential features in any teaching and learning of reading curriculum, if the learner is to be fully drawn inside and become a valuable participant in the learning process. Whilst it would probably be agreed by most teachers that 'a reader knows that learning to read is a lifelong process' might qualify as an important strand of learning, such a learning aim might not be a priority, and that the skills of 'intertextual relationships', or 'making predictions', are more important substantial goals to pursue.

Establishing a 'learning of reading' programme

An English department tackling the task of setting up a 'learning of reading' programme would need to start its deliberations based on the essential, or core, features of what it believes comprises 'reading'.

- It would need to devise a definition of reading with which it could feel most comfortable and which it considered most closely resembled its own attitudes and intentions. (The act of discussing such straightforward and fundamental issues would itself be an invaluable aid to improving learning in the department!)

- The team should then select those characteristics of 'being a reader', as illustrated in the examples above – or better alternatives that had been agreed by the department, if those I have suggested are regarded as unsuitable. These characteristics will become powerful 'drivers' of reading learning in the future, so they must have the full confidence and agreement of the department.

- On *every* occasion when lessons with an ostensible reading focus are planned in the future, the teacher would select at least one of the agreed characteristics/qualities to include and emphasise. The pupils would be made aware – as with all their learning intentions – that this feature should be given attention, and they would be expected to articulate for themselves how much progress is being made as a consequence. If pupils are being constantly reminded of these learning strands over the whole of their five-year secondary English course (and if colleagues in other subjects also gave due attention to them) it would be reasonable to expect that the relevant learning would have been sufficiently encouraged to make a real difference.

If six or so characteristics are chosen by a department, made explicit to the pupils over the entire period of Key Stages 3 and 4, given regular attention and assessment opportunities, there really should be clear learning taking place and real progress made during that period of every pupil's life.

From such considerations it is possible to construct very pointed and practical policies about reading. Whilst the characteristics noted already are vital to provide an effective learning centre for their work, the approaches and attitudes of the department should also be made manifestly clear. 'Policy', in this instance, very definitely means 'the shared agreed necessary practices of the team guiding everyday procedures, to be witnessed in all relevant lessons', not a collection of papers, stored in an unread file on a dusty shelf without any ultimate impact.

A model policy to be drawn from the characteristics/qualities included in the previous section might be:

We aim to enable all pupils to:

- know how important reading can be to literacy progression and the capacity to learn;

- read fluently and with understanding across the broadest possible range of textual material;

- know about a range of reading strategies, and to use independently all available clues in texts, to establish the most effective meaning-making;
- know that the makers of texts construct them for a variety of deliberate purposes, and for identifiable audiences;
- read for many different purposes (e.g. for pleasure, to find information, to establish models for own writing, to explore the views and attitudes of others, to compare messages and ideas in different media etc.);
- learn how to make realistic predictions about texts, and their structures, and to amend those predictions with the acquisition of further textual awareness;
- make progress as readers in a number of ways;
- become increasingly reflective about their own reading development, and to improve as monitors of their own progress.

Once a policy has been agreed for the English department, it should be easier to share those same principles with the other teachers in the school. If the policy is good enough to support the reading learning taking place in English, it should be quite capable of guiding the attitudes, approaches and activities being applied to reading in any circumstance in the school. In most 'reading events' taking place in lessons, most teachers have not given any attention or consideration to the issues of improving reading, or using the opportunity to improve learning in reading. Only by beginning to draw the attention of colleagues to the possibilities of 'using reading to develop reading', through the sharing of policies and procedures, can that school-wide possibility have a chance to become the normal practice.

Deciding reading priorities

As I pointed out in the previous chapter, there are a limited number of hours available for the whole secondary programme; only a proportion of that time can be dedicated to the teaching and learning of reading. It is therefore absolutely vital that the English department is clear about why any textual material selected has been included in the reading programme. No longer is it acceptable to include novels because, as I have heard teachers explain, 'I liked it and thought it would work with this class', or another instance I once saw in a school, where the Head of English informed me, 'We always read…in that term in Year 7'. If departments are to meet the legal requirement of the National Curriculum they already have the following texts decided for them, to be studied over the period of Key Stages 3 and 4:

- two plays by Shakespeare
- drama by major playwrights
- works of fiction by two major writers published before 1914 *[selected from a given list!]*
- two works of fiction by major writers published after 1914 *[thankfully, not selected from a given list]*
- poetry by four major poets published before 1914 *[also selected from a list]*
- poetry by four major poets published after 1914 *[only a suggestions list for this group]*
- recent and contemporary drama, fiction and poetry written for young people and adults
- drama, fiction and poetry by major writers from different cultures and traditions.

(DfEE/QCA 1999, my italics)

This list is then supplemented by 'non-fiction and non-literary texts', from a range which should 'include':

- literary non-fiction;
- print and ICT-based information and reference texts;
- media and moving image texts (for example, newspapers, magazines, advertisements, television, films and videos).

It is, of course, necessary to realise that the bulk of the actual day-to-day, real-life textual world of the vast majority of pupils in secondary schools is to be found in the very last, almost incidental, section.

It is my fervent hope that this particular set of curriculum requirements will be thoroughly re-thought and revised in the next curriculum review, whenever that is due, and pupils are offered a reading syllabus that has not been cobbled together from such a nakedly political 'literary heritage' viewpoint. Instead, schools should be offered a schedule that does not start very deliberately in the past (if texts determine their own agendas, this list has Shakespeare firmly at its head), where a textual here-and-now is apportioned grudgingly little more than the tiniest of space. It should be a programme that sets off from where pupils' textual interests and preoccupations are situated, and invites them to track back through a literary backdrop that they are entrusted and encouraged to shape in a number of possible and potentially exciting ways, to establish helpful context and extra layers of meaning. In the days before John Major's government so spitefully and arbitrarily reduced the status of coursework in the English GCSE, it was possible to visit classrooms and to see pupils of all abilities exploring and making textual relationships in just this imaginative manner. In the 'constructivist classrooms' described in the writing of Brooks and Brooks (1993), genuine learners are those who are practised and confident in raising their own questions and outlining their priority concerns in just this manner.

Nick Peim points out:

> Even though it may continue doggedly to make special claims for itself – special claims about its unique role in education – English takes up its place in the curriculum, being continuous with the systematic discrimination that is most crudely realized in exam procedures. It works against the majority of its students. English does this while proposing quite specific values and beliefs – about literacy, about the individual and about the world. These values and beliefs tend in general to devalue, or at least to exclude the cultural experiences of most of its subjects, or students.
>
> (Peim 1993)

We have an examination and national assessment system that is formulated on the notion of pupils overcoming certain hurdles at designated stages. If they cannot leap the hurdle, they are regarded as failing. As a recent commentator remarked, this situation is akin to expecting all 18-year-olds to take their driving test on their eighteenth birthday; if you pass, all well and good – fail, and you will not get a second chance. More sensible, and certainly more sensitive and motivating, is to embrace a system where pupils are entered for examinations and tests when they are ready for them. The test will then act as the official confirmation of the assessment reached in collaboration between pupil and teacher.

The former Chief Inspector of Schools, Mike Tomlinson, has recently offered to the government an interim report about the inadequacy of the current programme provided for 14- to 19-year-olds, as manifested in its examinations. His research, conducted in universities and schools, indicates that even the most able are deprived of certain essential skills that are required in the later levels of higher education. His recommendations should be taken extremely seriously and watched closely by English practitioners, as they are likely to impact upon the subject in fundamental ways. There are clear signs that his research is pointing to the introduction of a more 'basic skills' literacy-centred approach for large numbers of pupils post-14. The current assumptions about literature will be severely challenged, and there is no real indication that the textual engagements that pupils regularly encounter will be included in the programme of language, literacy and literary studies recommended to replace that currently seen in classrooms.

In the meantime, however, the existing Orders have to be recognised and complied with, although that does not mean that English departments merely accept that they have to work their way through the given list in unrelated, separate chunks of study, ticking them off as they go. If we bear in mind Shirley Clarke's advice, that the individual texts are to be thought of as the 'contexts' of any bigger learning projects, then it should be possible to weave an exciting and ambitious reading curriculum for Key Stages 3 and 4, even from the unpromising starting point of the present curriculum. The fundamental question for any English department to ask would be: whatever the requirements of textual coverage we are obliged to include, 'what are the major areas of textual learning and insight we would want our pupils to have successfully completed and grown in during their five-year programme of study in this school?' Every department should have established quite clear guiding principles for itself in relation to its core functions, in order to be in a position to ask this question. Effective long-term planning would be far easier to introduce after those principles were agreed, and the separate 'Key Learning Intentions' of the medium-term plan could then be apportioned to each year group in a progressive, cumulative development.

Determining an overview of learning intentions about reading

It is not unusual, as a result of asking English teachers what they are intending their pupils to learn from the study of texts in their classrooms before they begin a lesson, to be informed that they are exploring 'what they can find out about the characters', or 'the part the setting plays in the story', or 'how the plot works'. Much less often are teachers apparently concerned with the ways in which writers have used linguistic or structural devices or mannerisms to establish those characters or settings or plot outlines. Closer meaning-making understanding is not being regularly encouraged in these classroom interactions. This sort of situation comes about because texts, in this instance an individual novel, have too often been regarded as 'one-offs', self-standing pieces of material. Their broader relationships with other texts, or their place in a developmental continuum, have not been recognised and identified as the potentially necessary bigger learning picture. In a culture where, as Louise Stoll and her colleagues reminded us earlier: 'In a fast changing world, if you can't learn, unlearn and relearn, you're lost. Sustainable and continuous learning is a given of the twenty-first century.' (Stoll *et al.* 2003), it will be essential to learn more generally *about* textual material, to be able to apply that knowledge to the meaning-making processes of all texts.

Therefore, an English department devising a number of learning reading strands across a five-year programme might be thinking in terms of developing the whole notion of 'narrative'. Pupils will be 'introduced' (or at least asked to think more formally about narrative, as they will have been regularly acquainted with it in the previous six years of schooling) to the notion of 'narrative' in Year 7, and in the following four years will be systematically expected to revisit 'narrative' in progressive and more searching ways. It would, of course, be necessary to demonstrate that 'narrative', whilst a vital ingredient of most novels, is not exclusively to be found in that form of text. 'Narrative' seems to be the means that all human societies adopt to frame their events. Colin Harrison (Harrison 2004) refers to the seminal essay by Barbara Hardy, *The Cool Web*, published in 1977, in which she argued:

> that 'inner and outer storytelling' plays a major role in our sleeping and waking lives. She wrote 'For we dream in narrative, remember, hope, despair, believe, doubt, plan, revise, criticise, construct, gossip, learn, hate, and love by narrative. In order really to live, we make up stories about ourselves and others, about the personal as well as the social past and future.'
>
> The importance of narrative, she argues, is not simply about enjoyment of stories, or even about understanding ourselves. Narrative is a fundamental tool in the construction of intersubjectivity – the ability to recognise mental states in ourselves, and through imagination and projection to recognise the potential reciprocity of mental states in others – their beliefs, intentions, desires and the like – and it is this (and not simply the existence of language) that makes us distinctive as human beings.
>
> (Harrison 2004)

Rather than slavishly grinding their way through prescribed lists of texts in some form of 'checklist' manner, pupils should – it would seem from the enormity of the claim Harrison is repeating – be considering far more substantial matters, such as 'narrative', in their textual learning programmes. Rather than listing the different sorts of textual material to which pupils should be introduced, e.g. 'plays', 'poetry', 'works of prose fiction published before 1914', 'media and moving image texts', it would be far more challenging, and contribute to a broader learning understanding, if textual study could be organised in generic ways that can be detected through all forms of text, under headings such as 'narrative'.

Yet 'narrative' is just one possible cohering thematically related approach through which English teachers might want their pupils to make progress, and become more skilled in their learning journey through secondary school. Another approach, in which teachers of English are becoming increasingly confident, particularly since the introduction of the National Literacy Strategy and the Key Stage 3 English programme, is the study of textual 'genre', determined by the relationship of the purposes of texts, with their linguistic and organisational characteristics. So, in the future, pupils should be progressively able to identify and explain how the ways in which texts have been constructed contributes significantly to their intentions and meanings. From their earliest primary literacy lessons, pupils are being increasingly acquainted with the ways that, for instance, instructional, explanatory or persuasive textual material successfully fulfil their purposes because of the ways their linguistic and organisational features embody their 'fitness for purpose'. They could also be exploring the relationship of similar linguistic and purposeful aspects in the fictional (and poetic, dramatic and media) texts selected for their study. They might also be – in the early stages of secondary school – considering the properties that characterise 'action adventure', 'suspense' or 'horror' texts. As they grow older, pupils who have become confident in recognising these characteristics should be exploring, and increasingly able to recognise and understand, the features that denote more complex texts, as they interweave aspects of a number of genres, or express them more subtly.

Whatever the linking theme(s) of a reading curriculum adopted by a department, a better cohering overview than we currently see in most schools needs to be established. Pupils, in the main, are not able to see much connection in the various textual encounters in which they are invited to participate, nor do they understand what the elements of their own reading progression might be, in the same way that learning in mathematics or geography, for instance, feed back more obviously into future learning. The pupils do not readily make links across the materials they study, because much of it is being presented to them for a range of reasons that have little to do with a view of reading learning.

The expression of learning intentions related to reading

One of the ways that teachers might begin to contribute to a developing broader understanding of learning in reading would be to accustom their pupils to adopt textual approaches that encourage new and fresher ways of thinking about texts generally. This process can be aided by the way in which teachers formulate learning intentions. I regularly visit Key Stage 3 classrooms where (if they appear at all!) the 'learning intentions' (often called 'learning objectives') are expressed in the following typical terms:

> L.O. 'to describe the characters in [name of text]', or L.O. 'to write the front page of a tabloid newspaper', or L.O. 'to read poems about war', or L.O. 'to compare simple and complex sentences' [all real examples].

What is immediately obvious about those examples is that they are *activities*, not learning issues. Whilst they might represent necessary concerns at the earliest stages of study, to ensure that some sort of relationship is being made with the text, they do not ultimately enable pupils to become more knowledgeable about a broader platform of textual matters. The pupils are given no guidance in these circumstances of what they should *do* intellectually with the study they have conducted. They need more guidance about the manner in which the study they are currently conducting relates to raising important questions of all texts. They need to be exercised in other ways, encouraged to think much more widely, as in the first example quoted above, around the whole possible notion of 'characters'. Why are characters necessary? How are characters deployed by different authors? What sorts of possibilities or difficulties do authors encounter in their use of characters? Are there texts in which characters are of lesser significance than other, more important, features? In short, the overall 'key learning intention' ought to involve a much fuller consideration of the wider topic of 'characters'. The whole study unit embracing this topic would then need shaping in such a way as to ensure that pupils encountered different sorts of characters, or became familiar with characters appearing to perform different functions in a range of textual circumstances. Given the huge range of possible ways of setting up a worthwhile learning reading curriculum, this is just one suggested possible fragment of that potential programme.

Teachers should also be in tune with the issues of continuity, and the appropriate expectations of their pupils as they arrive in the secondary school. Whatever many secondary teachers think of the National Literacy Strategy in primary schools (and many are still suspicious of its apparent constraints and perceived over-emphasis on the teaching of language (Goodwyn 2004; Marshall 2002)), they cannot deny that there has been a sea-change in the knowledge of the vast majority of primary teachers since the introduction of the Strategy in 1998 (Ofsted 2004). This transformation has meant that many pupils are arriving in Year 7 with a more mature understanding of text, and the more able are capable of raising a level of questioning once unheard of in the early stages of Key Stage 3. The following are learning intentions I saw recently in the medium-term plans of Year 4 in a middle school:

i.   To know the metalangue associated with poetry and to be able to discuss personal poetry preferences using that knowledge;
ii. To know the conventions, and linguistic and organisational features of instructional texts; to demonstrate that knowledge by creating similar examples of those texts;
iii. To understand how settings and character are built from small details and to demonstrate that knowledge by writing character sketches and examples of settings in similar ways.

If Year 4 children are capable of engaging successfully with such intentions (and they patently are, as my own observations have proved), and increase their knowledge significantly as a result, their secondary teachers have to be ready to engage them at commensurate levels when they begin their secondary English courses. The evidence of pupil underachievement during Key Stage 3, because they are often insufficiently challenged, is very clear from the work of researchers such as Jean Ruddock and her colleagues at Cambridge (Ruddock *et al.* 1996).

Rethinking the 'framing' of learning intentions could become a powerful starting point in setting up a proper level of challenge for new Year 7 pupils, particularly those who have already experienced more focused planning in their primary schools.

The following are examples of secondary English learning intentions I have seen being planned by teachers of pupils in Key Stages 3 and 4:

i. Year 7 – To know that 'gothic horror' texts are recognisable by the following characteristics:…and to demonstrate that knowledge by identifying these features in unfamiliar examples of the genre;

ii. Year 8 – To understand that good readers are capable of raising a series of sentence-level questions whilst reading texts, and to be able to raise new and searching questions of my own;

iii. Year 9 /10 – To know that modern narrative texts are constructed in ways that deliberately make them less 'realistic' than similar sorts of texts from other literary periods.

Pupils familiar with these sorts of overview Key Learning Intentions are much more likely to be able to recognise the potential 'success criteria' being expected through such an approach, and will better articulate to themselves the sorts of outcomes they are striving to achieve – and to understand what counts as real success. The means of making assessment of learning is also made much clearer, to teachers and pupils, as a result of this shared discourse. If the pupils are expected to 'know' or 'understand' more specific features of textual matter, then teachers will be seeking the extent to which that knowledge or understanding has been demonstrated, and pupils will realise where the focus of their responses ought to be situated.

Useful areas of reading planning can be constructed on the following model learning intentions:

a. to know the typical (linguistic, structural, narrative characteristics of…[an author], [a genre], [a period of time];

b. To know how characters are established and developed in…[an author's work etc.];

c. To know the main concerns being explored by…in their novels/ stories/publications/television programmes etc.;

d. To understand how a range of meanings are made through the different structural devices in the poems of…;

e. To be able to understand and explain the dramatic features of…;

f. To know [e.g. distinctive features etc. of two different authors] and to compare and contrast how they impact on the reader (e.g. make different effects);

g. To show understanding of the social issues of [a particular time] and how [an author's work etc.] might be seen as deliberately challenging…

Knowing the most appropriate questions to ask about reading

The *Framework for Teaching English: Years 7, 8 and 9* (DfEE 2001a) reminds English teachers of the possibility of approaching the understanding of textual material from three different standpoints: text-level, sentence-level and word-level. These are not new procedures, but they have not regularly been part of the ways much learning has been structured in the past. Pupils of all abilities can benefit from the potential of this way of asking questions of any sort of text, if they have sufficiently practised the straightforward but incisive techniques involved. The real challenge is to make this approach utterly systematic for all pupils, so they readily move into this set of critical modes when confronting unfamiliar textual materials.

At **text level**, pupils should be ready to ask the following sorts of questions:

- Why have I been expected to engage with this text? (Has my teacher given it to me for a purpose I understand? Have I chosen it to fulfil certain information-seeking requirements? Have I heard of this text from sources I trust? Am I giving myself a challenge? etc.)

- Are there aspects of this text about which I can immediately make sense? (Is this text accessible to me? Which features of the text are making engagement difficult? What might I need to sort out to make better progress with this text? etc.)

- Does this text resemble other texts I have encountered previously? (Can I recognise ideas, matters of language/layout/organisation, content etc. that allow me to make a more immediate orientation with this text?)

- Can I work out the purpose of this text? (Is it possible quickly to establish what this text is doing by its title, its language, its presentation, where I came across it, etc.?)

- Can I find my way around this text to discover whatever it is I want from it? (Do I know what the sections are for? Can I use the subheadings? Do I know what the pictures are contributing to the meaning?)

- What am I expected to do as a result of this reading encounter? (Do I think about the material/ideas/themes? Should I make notes? Do I need to rework the material to make a presentation for a different audience?)

- Do I like this sort of material?

At the **sentence level**, readers need to bring their knowledge of language to the questions they put to the text. This has often been an area of consideration not given the amount of attention it deserves. The linguist George Keith, in his chapter 'Noticing Grammar' in the QCA publication *Not Whether but How – Teaching Grammar in English at Key Stages 3 and 4* (QCA 1999) makes a wholly convincing case for looking closely at the language of texts for the fullest meaning-making. In my book *Grammar for Improving Writing and Reading in the Secondary School* (Dean 2003), and Debra Myhill's *Better Writers* (2001), there are many more examples of the ways in which paying close attention to the grammar of texts can enable pupils to make much better progress in understanding the meanings of texts. In one particular exercise I recommend, pupils are expected to read and consider closely each individual word as it is revealed. They are asked to discuss its fullest implications – perhaps its function in a 'word class' context, the issues and ideas that might be associated with it, the possible surprises it might cause (or not) – as a way of making a close relationship between reader and text. We could not, of course, read in this way all the time, but as an occasional exercise through which pupils would be expected to improve their skills it has the potential to offer a very substantial development of learning.

Examples of fundamental sentence level questions might be:

- How dense or difficult is this text? (Is the text written in straightforward, easy language, or do I have trouble making immediate meaning from the words?)

- What is the average sentence length? (Are the sentences in this text short, tight and direct, or are they long, with multiple examples of punctuation, or somewhere in between?)

- Is there a variety of sentence type? (Are all the sentences statements, or are some in questions? Is the exclamatory used? Are the sentence patterns very similar, or is it possible to see differences?)

- Are there any special effects in the language being used for particular purposes, and can I identify those purposes? (Do some of the sentences have no verb? Is ellipsis employed? Do some sentences resemble speech?)

- Who or what is the narrator of this text, and through which linguistic effects is the 'voice' of the text recognisable?

- What is the prevailing tone or attitude of this text? (Is it serious and formal, distant and high-minded, or light-hearted and jolly – or various combinations of these alternatives?)

At the **word level**, pupils are being asked to 'notice' the vocabulary, the lexis of the text, through the following sorts of questions:

- Are the words of the text familiar, or are a proportion of them difficult or unknown?

- Is the vocabulary consistent, or does it change in identifiable sections, for particular purposes?

- Is it possible to determine the intended audience from the chosen vocabulary?

- Are certain words or expressions used for special purposes?
- Does the 'sound' of the words contribute to the meaning of the text?
- Are the words of our time or from earlier times in history?
- Are there examples of puns, irony, overstatement or other forms of humour?
- Is the language formal or informal, or at some stage between the two extremes?

Becoming familiar with these questions and growing increasingly confident in their application are concrete learning aspects of reading that should be within the reach of virtually every pupil. Departments adopting a view of progression in these approaches to textual understanding will ensure that their classes become secure at each stage, and by the end of their courses will expect those readers to be utterly assured in approaching unfamiliar material with a strong repertoire of critical tools.

Changing the teaching of reading to the learning of reading

One of the biggest complaints from English teachers and others concerned with the subject since the introduction of the National Literacy Strategy in 1998 and the secondary English programme within the Key Stage 3 Strategy, introduced in 2001, has been the apparent diminution in importance of reading whole texts (Thomas 2001; Allen 2002; Pullman 2002; Goodwyn 2004). Neither strategy, it ought to be stressed, actually requires the study of extracts or sections of whole texts, rather than whole texts, but many teachers have felt that meeting the demands of the strategies to consider a much broader range of texts than has been expected in the past can only be met through such a 'bitty' approach.

Some part of this problem has arisen, I would suggest, from the way that departments have traditionally been resourced, and that it is time for a reappraisal of these issues, if creative solutions are to be made possible. In virtually every secondary English department I have ever visited, the teachers have purchased a number of sets of 'class readers' for study purposes. So, everybody in the class has been expected to read exactly the same text, usually at the same pace, until it is finished, whilst a number of pieces of writing, or dramatic or speaking activities have been conducted on it.

In *Teaching Reading in Secondary Schools* (Dean 2000/3) I suggested that this way of dealing with fictional texts in the English classroom was unsatisfactory for a number of reasons, and I explored alternative approaches. One other way to tackle this issue might be for the department to decide on a suitable genre for study – such as 'suspense', 'historical' or 'magic realism' – and then to purchase a number of copies of four/five examples of the genre. All pupils in the class would be expected to engage with the generic features which constitute that genre, as introductory study, with respect to all the examples of the genre that they have available. They should read the first few pages, even the first chapter, of each of the examples, finally choosing the text they would wish to continue reading to its end. The teacher would not then read with the whole class, but would direct and model analytical study in broad terms, applicable to all the selected examples being read by four or five groups in the room. The pupils, in groups relating to their selected texts, would, of course, continue their reading, and be expected to contribute back into the collaborative sessions, making reference to their particular texts.

In this arrangement, the teacher would actually be teaching not one text, but four or five, and the pupils would be in a better position to understand the relationship between numbers of texts with supposedly similar characteristics. They would also, by proxy, be acquainted with rather more texts than would be achieved merely by reading a single class text. Teachers could use this approach to differentiate the reading in the classroom, if they wished, although I believe that personal pupil choice ought to be the real advantage to exploit. I also think that this way of dealing with a text is more likely to lead to pupils developing their own independent reading practices; they will, after all, have chosen the text for themselves, they can be given themes and issues to pursue in their own example of the genre, and they can work in a supportive group in a sort of 'reading club'. They might also be interested enough in what they hear about the texts they have not actually chosen to read them independently, thus extending their personal range of self-managed reading.

Such an approach would mean that a department would have to think differently about its resource purchasing, and would probably mean – given the currently large collections of single novels in most English store cupboards – that the practice could only be gradually introduced. It would also mean that English teachers would need to read more, to know what the possible related texts in any genre collection might be, although I would not regard that point as in any way disadvantageous.

Rethinking ways of bringing pupils to texts, and encouraging the deepening of that relationship, is something that English teachers should be expected to do, more than other colleagues responsible for other subjects. Yet, the main issue is not just about the enjoyment young people come by as a result of those associations with texts – although any pleasure that can be encouraged through these engagements is to be welcomed and celebrated. The biggest concern of all teachers really should focus on the *learning of reading* that has resulted. The only ways of being sure that good learning has gone on is, of course, to have reliable systems of assessment that actually relate to the original learning intentions.

The assessment of reading

Testing and assessing reading has been a problem for secondary schools for almost as long as they have been concerned about its teaching. One of the strangest anomalies about reading assessment has been that it is usually undertaken through writing exercises. Only the youngest of schoolchildren, learning to read for the first time, are regularly 'tested' by being encouraged to read aloud to an adult. Virtually everybody from Year 7 onwards is either asked questions, usually of a tightly closed nature, in their lessons, to check that the text has been 'comprehended', or they are subjected to a written exercise, sometimes extended, but occasionally focused, to investigate whether the textual material being studied has been sufficiently well understood.

Colin Harrison, Professor of Literacy Studies at Nottingham University, in a recent important book, *Understanding Reading Development*, develops a theme about challenging the nature of reading 'comprehension' that has concerned him for some years:

> This reassessment of the concept of meaning, of the role of the reader and of the authority in text, raises profound questions about the nature of reading assessment, particularly in its traditional forms, and it is these questions which have led me to the bold formulation that there is no such thing as reading comprehension, at least, not as we have often been inclined to understand it – as a steady state of knowledge formed in the reader's mind following the reading of a text. I have given children reading comprehension exercises, tried to develop their reading comprehension, and have used the phrase to refer to what readers understand from what they have read, but I think it is important, too, to remind ourselves that reading comprehension processes are elusive, evanescent, and in many respects, inaccessible.
>
> (Harrison 2004)

Harrison claims that it is not possible 'to investigate someone's reading comprehension without affecting the nature of their response', which, if true, means that we have to be prepared radically to rethink the nature of assessment activities that have been apparently unproblematically accepted by many as capable of making valid judgement on children's reading abilities. And he continues:

> I want to suggest that, most of the time at least, we haven't yet dared to or had the imagination to consider the implications for assessing response to reading, or measuring reading comprehension, of the postmodern positions we adopt as teachers. There's a chasm between the liberal positions of our pedagogy and the coercive positions of our assessment mechanisms and the assumptions which underpin them, and at the very least it is important to recognise this, and to set ourselves the agenda of bridging the chasm.
>
> (ibid.)

Harrison goes further. He states that:

> the National Curriculum in England and Wales currently presents an ultimately damaging model of assessment, and that if teachers were permitted to move towards a portfolio system within which evidence of reading activity was collected according to the principles of Responsive Assessment, then most of the problems associated with National Curriculum assessment would evaporate.
>
> (ibid.)

I have long had sympathy with the position so clearly articulated by Harrison. The current means of assessment, embodied in the SATs tests conducted at the conclusion of Key Stages 2 and 3, are the worst form of superficial judgement, however hard the curriculum assessment agencies have tried to vary them and give them broader applicability. This long accepted means of testing, has, in turn, led to a far greater concern with the child's interactions with individual texts, rather than with each child's growth as a 'reader', which I believe to be far more important and, ultimately, the really vital overall aim of the teaching of reading. Teachers of reading must have authentic insight into the way any reader is drawing on, and aware of, the range of reading meaning-making strategies available to every child, because, in the long run, these should be the areas of focused attention resulting from the assessment made of them.

A major problem associated with the teaching of reading, certainly during the last 30 years, but probably for longer, has been the lack of robust, adequate formative assessment procedures capable of describing ongoing pupil progression. Very few departments would be able to articulate with any real certainty how their pupils are developing as readers or what improvements are being brought about in their personal responses to the texts with which they are engaging. These problems have not been solved with any confidence in English departments in relation to the reading of fiction texts, which are, after all, the staple content of English study; they have been virtually wholly neglected in relation to non-fiction texts.

I have been encouraging teachers to adopt other, complementary, forms of reading assessment for some years. A very simple model is illustrated in Figure 4.1. This 'mind map' of the reader serves a number of purposes very simply, but yields important information to the monitoring adults. The example offered need not be the only version that departments use with their pupils; it merely offers a possible picture.

Pupils, given a copy of this sheet, are asked to write their names in the middle of a plain sheet of paper. They then draw lines, equivalent to those on the sheet leading to questions, and substitute bullet-point answers where the questions appear on the original paper. Part of the purpose of the exercise is to avoid pupils writing long answers, so they should be encouraged to make them as direct and

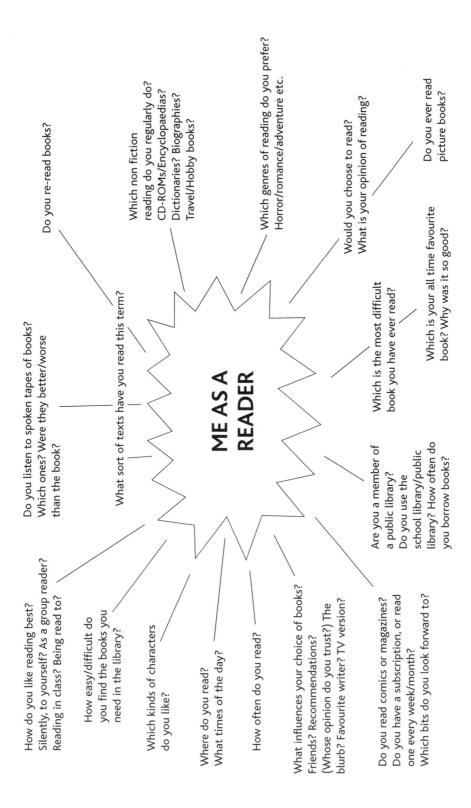

Do you re-read books?

Which non fiction
reading do you regularly do?
CD-ROMs/Encyclopaedias?
Dictionaries? Biographies?
Travel/Hobby books?

Which genres of reading do you prefer?
Horror/romance/adventure etc.

Would you choose to read?
What is your opinion of reading?

Do you ever read
picture books?

Do you listen to spoken tapes of books?
Which ones? Were they better/worse
than the book?

What sort of texts have you read this term?

**ME AS A
READER**

Which is the most difficult
book you have ever read?

Which is your all time favourite
book? Why was it so good?

How do you like reading best?
Silently, to yourself? As a group reader?
Reading in class? Being read to?

How easy/difficult do
you find the books you
need in the library?

Which kinds of characters
do you like?

Where do you read?
What times of the day?

How often do you read?

What influences your choice of books?
Friends? Recommendations?
(Whose opinion do you trust?) The
blurb? Favourite writer? TV version?

Do you read comics or magazines?
Do you have a subscription, or read
one every week/month?
Which bits do you look forward to?

Are you a member of
a public library?
Do you use the
school library/public
library? How often do
you borrow books?

Figure 4.1 Mind map of the vendor

short as possible. This exercise could be quickly administered as pupils arrive in the secondary school in September, undertaken again at half term, in October, and the end of the term, in December. Further exercises can be spread across the rest of the school year, so that at least six pieces of evidence are collected in this particular portfolio across that period. Teachers should, of course, maintain a monitoring interest in these pieces of paper, looking out for signs of development and change. Where pupils' answers remain static, the teachers should be alerted to intervene, and to offer help and advice through discussion. I also believe that every pupil in Year 7 deserves at least one reading interview with a 'reading mentor' – whatever the ability or attainment of the reader – and these sheets would offer a genuine starting point for a worthwhile discussion.

Secondary teachers should also be ready to explore the potential of **reading logs** or **reading journals**. These booklets, requiring no more investment than simple exercise books, are a means of setting up a dialogue between the reader and an adult mentor – probably, but not necessarily, the English teacher. They could be developed in any way the teacher, or – even better – the individuals in any class decide. Pupils are encouraged to write as little or as much as they wish, about any aspect of the texts in which they are currently involved. They might explore why the text was chosen; what they anticipate about their relationship with it; any predictions, disappointments, highlights, unexpected pleasures or intertextual insights etc. The teacher, or mentor, reads the journals regularly, but does not 'mark' them. They can comment or question or otherwise take part in a dialogue, but they do not make judgements on what the pupil has written. Developed carefully, these documents can become an extremely valuable way of tracing pupils' growth and increasing maturity and sophistication as writers. They can become manageable homework, and in many circumstances I have seen otherwise reluctant writers ready to add a few lines to their journals.

Teachers regularly bemoan the difficulties they encounter in encouraging their male pupils to read independently. The two suggestions outlined above are not offered as certain ways of solving such predicaments, but they have the potential for re-engaging boys as readers, without placing too much pressure on them, and allow them to make progress in independent reading at their own pace. They also allow the learners a genuine voice in their development – absolutely essential prerequisites in ensuring that learners are likely to stay involved.

Assessment of reading also tends to diminish during the period of secondary education. Pupils in Key Stage 3 are given more attention, in pure reading terms, than their senior counterparts in Key Stage 4, where the reading is assumed to be either 'in place', or pupils are regarded as not very able in the area of reading. Teachers should be ensuring that reading progress continues into Years 10 and 11, and the sorts of suggestions made above could encourage that development to take place without too much extra bureaucracy and difficult arrangement.

Problems of learning with poetry

> Poetry presents particular problems for teachers and students alike in that it is not widely read and – like Shakespeare – comes at the bottom of young people's preferences in reading literature; the language or diction of poetry is often seemingly impenetrable; the range of poems studied is often narrow; it is taught in conventional ways that presupposes the purpose of teaching is to elucidate 'difficult' language and for students to gain appreciation of 'high culture'; and it is often reduced to a hunt for similes and metaphors, as if they were the *sine qua non* of poetry (when in fact they are the features of many different types of writing.)
>
> (Andrews 2001)

Richard Andrews has clearly visited many of the same sorts of English classrooms as myself. Poetry is so often presented as some sort of special gourmet dish, requiring particular forms of well-developed tastebuds to detect the subtly hidden flavours. It is little wonder that pupils are then unready or unwilling to apply their normal everyday skills to be prepared to make meanings in the usual manner of most textual encounters, before moving on to a further level of questioning. Having a mature sense of making meaning, whatever the context, is the important first factor for pupils attempting to make any sort of progress with poetry.

So teachers may agree with Aristotle, that 'poetry is more philosophical and of higher value than history', or Matthew Arnold, that 'genuine poetry is conceived in the soul', or even with Wordsworth, that 'poetry is the breath and finer spirit of all knowledge: it is the impassioned expression which is in the countenance of all Science'. But these are not starting points for wanting to become involved and engaged in the material of poetry. Coleridge suggests that 'Prose = words in their best order; poetry = the best words in the best order', and English teachers have to enable pupils to adopt positions relative to poetry that allows them to both understand what Coleridge is positing, and to come to a position where they can judge his claim for themselves.

Just as it is not, ultimately, very helpful in the larger order of things to spend too much time in the English reading curriculum concentrating on single works, so it is with the study of poetry. Andrews recommends 'extending the range of poems read in class beyond those informed by the ideology of "emotion recollected in tranquillity"' (Andrews 2001). Pupils need to become familiar with the broadest possible range of poems, from the mundane and undemanding to the obscure, to develop an overriding sense of the 'poetic'; to see where poetry can be employed and why, and to begin recognising that most fundamental starting point in the understanding of poetry – that it is not prose. I still see too many less confident language users approaching poetry in their lessons as if the peculiar layout of the poetic texts they are studying is merely a perverse typographical error. To become 'bold' in the face of poetry, pupils need to see and read aloud many examples of different poets, to acquaint themselves with the huge variety of rhythms, voices, expression and viewpoints that are situated within such works.

Too often, in English classrooms, poems are approached from 'special' positions, as if they are not composed of language in the same way that other texts are. They might, as Coleridge describes them, be 'the best words in the best order', but they are, after all, conveyed in words, and there has to be careful attention paid to those words to decide by what criteria the order they have been placed in could be regarded as 'the best'. Readers of the poems need to be enquiring why the work they are considering is regarded as 'poetry' and not 'prose'. They should be asking serious questions about the intent of the poet, in the same way as they might be asking about the intent of a crusading journalist or the intent of the advertising agency responsible for creating a promotional leaflet. The biggest difficulty for the unaccustomed reader of poetry to overcome is about tuning to the 'inner voice', that voice in the head that experienced readers are capable of hearing, alerting them to the rhythms and cadences of poetic styles, when consciously reading a piece of unfamiliar poetic text. Good readers can slip into a sort of intellectual role-play exercise when confronted with difficult texts, to 'test' which might seem most suitable in any particular context. These skills can be taught, and pupils can learn to explore and extend the repertoire of 'voices' on which they should be able to draw.

In my book *Grammar for Improving Writing and Reading in the Secondary School* (Dean 2003), already referred to in a previous section (page 92), I suggest ways by which pupils can be supported in developing a technique I call 'close linguistic study'. This technique can be applied just as effectively to poetry as with prose text. Indeed, in some instances, pupils should be helped to attend closely to the language and grammar of the piece before attempting to 'work out what it is about'. Looking at the vocabulary, for instance, can reveal patterns of words, or associations that can offer clues to the meaning. If, after having built up a 'scaffold' of solid linguistic observations, the reader then asks some questions of the 'evidence' accrued, better speculation about the areas of interest of the poem is likely. Learners also need to be familiar with the 'technical vocabulary' of poetry, such as 'irony', 'imagery' and 'symbol', to realise that language has the capabilities of playing tricks, standing in for other ideas or being representative of whole concepts. It is often claimed that girls and boys tend to respond to poetry differently, in ways determined along gender lines. I tend to believe that is a very superficial finding, relating only to initial responses. Given much of the critical armoury outlined above, and some appropriate staging points in the approaches made to poetry, all pupils can be enabled to face the problems of meaning-making in poetry study, and to build effective ways of tackling them by practising in contexts where solid 'learning intentions' guide the work.

So a teacher might enable a group of pupils to consider more widely the many possible effects taking place through the medium of poetry by focusing very specifically on such issues as:

- To know that poets use irony as a way of making more powerful comment on their subject (or… as a way of making the reader see a different perspective on a subject etc.);
- To know that poets can comment on events in a personal way, or by adopting a third person viewpoint;
- To know that (a) poet(s) can make certain sorts of meaning (or comment) through the patterns of sound in the poem.

' "Literary studies lead constantly outside themselves", as Leavis puts it' (DES 1975).

In encouraging a stronger and more focused attitude on reading learning, I am never sidelining or dismissing the power of individual relevance and personal enjoyment. The tighter teaching and learning approach I have advocated in this chapter, and in *Teaching Reading in Secondary Schools* (Dean 2000/2003), has come about because of my perception that too few young people in secondary schools are properly engaged on worthwhile reading journeys, in which they have inadequate or insecure starting places. It is not unlike watching those who wish to ride a horse looking for a box or other aid on which to climb to be in a position to swing a leg over and become properly seated on the saddle. Until the rider is comfortable the proper riding cannot begin and the horse will wheel about under no real control.

I have no doubts that when readers are fully drawn into the reading process they are then capable of exponentially setting off other potentially valuable extra dimensions that skilled readers expect and rely upon as part of their full reading experiences. Good readers, for instance, know that they bring the whole of their previous 'literacy biographies', and all that has taken place in their perceived lives, to the matter they are reading, adding meaning to it in unique ways. They know what it is to be carried away into the 'silent core' of reading:

> I never heard it, this extra degree of hush that somehow travelled through walls and ceilings to announce that my seven-year self had become about as absent as a present person could be. The silence went both ways. As my concentration on the story in my hands took hold, all sounds faded away. My ears closed. I didn't imagine the process of the cut-off like a shutter dropping, or as a narrowing of the pink canals leading

inside each waxy cartilaginous passage irising tight like some alien doorway in *Star Trek*.

(Spufford 2002)

They know how the matters dealt with in texts (fiction and non-fiction) can touch triggers inside themselves, and they know how exciting and enthralling following through narratives and issues can be. Above all, they know that there are different sorts of enjoyment to be had in reading. Yet a considerable number of 'readers' do not start at these points. Just as many pupils fail to become readers at all. That is why a systematic, analytical, skills-based, text-centred reading programme has to be *learned* by so many.

> The most fundamental aspect of learning to read is not about skills; it is about learning to behave like a reader. Successful readers pick up books, curl up with them on a bean bag, worry or get excited about what is going to happen to characters in a story, and later talk spontaneously about what they have been reading to their parents or their friends...
>
> But as well as having experience of a social context in which books are valued, beginning readers need at least four other kinds of knowledge: knowledge of how the world works, knowledge of how language works, knowledge of how stories work and knowledge of how a book works...

(Harrison 2004)

The enjoyment of reading for a considerable part of the population begins with teaching and learning, it is not the beginning of the reading process.

> The conclusion seems difficult to avoid that if English teachers are to achieve the ambitious goals described in progressive and radical educational writing, they must reconsider the functions of knowledge and the traditional skills of literacy. If pupils of all abilities are to become seriously engaged with the examination of controversial issues, to arrive at critical perspectives on established institutions, they must posses the relevant information and appropriate tools of enquiry. Exclusive attention to enjoyment and interest can trivialise issues, confine children to their own experience, with all the inequalities within this which they bring to school and put the teachers' confidence and effectiveness at risk.

(Mathieson 1975)

Improving learning in writing

Much of our professional attention as teachers has been directed towards the kinds of writing tasks we set – towards drawing on the child's experiences or establishing appropriate audiences or purposes for writing. In summary, teachers have – at different times – overemphasised correctness, overemphasised personal response, and overemphasised form. Although there has been much valuable work on how to mark and assess children's writing, there has been almost no attention given to how to intervene during writing and how to be active in teaching writing. Put simply, we set up writing tasks and we mark writing, but we do little to help writers understand how to write better.

(Myhill 2001)

I would go further than Debra Myhill, in her searching examination of writing practices in secondary English, and suggest that one of the major problems teachers face in their classrooms is that, despite all the attention of such national movements as the Literacy Strategy and other huge areas of writing focus, many of the pupils quite simply have no idea why they are being asked to write in the first place. For thousands of pupils, writing is an activity that is unthinkingly associated with 'one of those things' that people do at school; one of those accepted, barely understood activities that fills the day and passes the time between eight-thirty and three-thirty. Considerable numbers of young people set off on writing exercises in lessons of all sorts without a sense of what they are attempting to achieve, and particularly without a notion of what a successful piece of writing – what it is they should be attempting to achieve – may actually be like. They are unable to muster a sufficiently clear overview of what it is they are expected to demonstrate in the written medium. Part of this problem is the result of what sometimes goes on in English itself, but much of it rests firmly with the pointlessness of huge amounts of writing expected of pupils in all other areas of the school, which regularly fail to supply the insights needed so vitally by these potential writers.

Many commentators on literacy (Myhill 2001; Graves 1983; Sheeran and Barnes 1991; Beard 2001) stress how difficult writing can be. It is one of the most demanding activities that humans undertake. The writer is often compared with the talker, and writing is unequivocally regarded as being the more demanding. Talking (except on the telephone and, more recently, in video-conferencing) usually means that the communicator is in the presence of the receiver: meanings can be clarified; expression helps advance meaning; tone and volume are purposefully regulated in the exchange, and the whole discourse is dependent on and subject to the relationships between the participants, which are usually understood on both sides. Writing is often undertaken solitarily; difficult ideas have to be captured accurately in words that are often capable of other interpretations on the page, without the writer able to make the precise meanings clear; tone and attitude have to be carefully minded; punctuation is usually vital for precision; meanings, whether intended or not, become fixed by the reader without possibility of flexibility. What has been written can depend on the mood, context or other matters affecting the reader's experience. In school terms, the reader (usually a teacher) is almost always a better writer than the pupil, and is not much affected by what has been written, but is greatly concerned with the manner of its construction.

It is also worth exploring what sorts of writing typically take place in English classrooms. Much writing is set up to show that pupils have understood reading matter of some sort, either through related activities (e.g. a 'wanted' poster of a character from a novel, the front page of The Verona Times, a written character study, or the comparison of two poems) or pastiche, in the form of an alternative ending to a text, or even the 'addition' of another chapter. In these extremely common circumstances it can be seen that the important criteria of actually improving writing can regularly play a lesser role than the details that have been included in the piece, and this impression stays with the pupils without being challenged. In Key Stage 3 there is often encouragement of autobiographical writing, perhaps some description ('The View from My Bedroom Window') and occasional ventures into narrative and storytelling. During the last two or three years there has been an upsurge of genre-based, non-fiction writing in secondary classrooms, as a result of a trend encouraged in the National Literacy Strategy in primary schools.

Key Stage 4 writers relate most of their writing in English to the study of texts for GCSE purposes (still much of it focused on a broad understanding of reading 'comprehension'), with some pieces searching the pupils' understanding of how to structure and pursue such genres as discussion or persuasion. Considerable numbers of pupils at that stage write short essays, commenting on a feature of a poem, prose piece or play, to 'prove' that they have had acquaintance with it, enabling it, duly, to take its place in a coursework folder as evidence. There is a tightly limited functional feel to the business of writing in English in schools, most types of which most pupils will never repeat or revisit once they have finished statutory education.

> Writing is routinely used as the medium for learning and for assessment at all stages of the educational system and, as such, it ceases to be the immediate focus of attention. Whilst the writing may well be corrected for superficial accuracy in spelling or punctuation, the principal assessment focus is concerned with the extent to which the writing indicates, for example, understanding of a literary text or historical period. The sheer amount of writing children produce during their time in school has often been noticed...but only on rare occasions is the writing itself made the focus of teaching attention.
>
> (Myhill 2001)

Whilst recent research (QCA 2004, unpublished) indicates that writing achievement, at least as far as it is measured in test terms, improves as pupils pass through the secondary school, there is no real evidence to show that pupils actually know more about writing as they grow older. A huge amount of school-based writing is routine and fails to contribute to learning. A proportion of young people arrive at school practised in the sorts of literacy backgrounds that will contribute to effective writing, but for the majority writing is too often a virtually meaningless activity. Standards of punctuation, spelling and cohesion remain a real cause for concern, and will continue to resist all current classroom attention to those issues until pupils are more prepared to take greater responsibility for their writing, involve themselves in writing because they recognise how importantly it is serving particular personal and learning purposes, and, as a result of their commitment to their work, they feel genuinely impelled to convey more precise meanings and want to improve.

Once again, developing a sense in all pupils of what it means to be an 'independent learner' can be seen to be a vital prerequisite of bringing about effective learning in an area of English. As real 'learners' in the whole-school context, pupils should be expected to negotiate their learning programmes in a mature and genuinely shared partnership with their 'learning managers', and – absolutely necessarily – *want* to convey what they have learned and to explore what they are learning through substantial, valued writing practices that are regarded by the writers themselves as authentic. 'Writing' will be wholly contextually appropriate as a natural part of the learning process in such circumstances; in such circumstances 'writers' will be taking real responsibility for their written efforts, and will press themselves to achieve the accuracy and precision these activities will demand. But those factors can only be possible in a future where good learning behaviours are promoted, where personal responsibility is understood and accepted and where the apparatus of the learning institution – people, resources and environment – are dedicated to such developments.

I recently came across the work of a group of Year 7 pupils taking part in an authentic research programme, the Children's Research Centre, based at the Open University. The pupils were taught how to research, the methodologies and ethics of research etc., and shown how research has to make a difference to what is known in the world. They then undertake a piece of research of their own choosing, and write it up. The writing demands of this programme are extremely demanding, but the pupils are more than ready to learn the writing skills that will best represent and enhance their findings. With genuinely important matters to convey, they need genuinely fine-tuned appropriate ways to express them.

In the meantime, we have a national state of affairs where most English teachers continue to read regularly and enjoy reading after graduation, and many model that enthusiasm to their classes. Yet few English teachers write for pleasure, or give any sense of personal enthusiasm for writing. Fewer still actually join their pupils in writing enterprises, either to share and better understand the problems, or to offer substantial exemplar material. Denied this close-up demonstration of the craft of writing, pupils have attempted to move through the writing process without the 'structure' of the important stages fully in place in their own approaches. Potential writers have also, traditionally in the past, been denied access to the vital craft materials – i.e. the knowledge of and working control over fundamental areas of grammar – to make the sorts of decisions in respect of their writing which would act as indicators of growing control and progression.

Huge attention has been paid, during the past decade, to the writing of boys, many of whom have recognised the pointlessness of what they have been asked to perform at an early stage of their writing development, and refuse to commit to it further. But the problem is not a straightforward one, explained merely through gender differences. Many girls, on the evidence from my own classroom observations, are as uncertain about why they should, and how to, write as their male classmates, and their learning and development is often as slow.

All the matters mentioned above, amongst others, have hindered the development of 'learning' in writing and require serious attention before change and improvement are likely to take place. Teachers need to be more secure about teaching writing in circumstances where they are confident that what their pupils are learning from those exercises will be of long-lasting and necessary value in all aspects of their immediate *and* later lives. Pupils need to be clear about why they are being asked to undertake the sorts of writing exercises required of them, and what their own part in them needs to be to ensure that appropriate progression and growth continue.

New directions in the teaching of literacy brought about by the introduction of the Literacy Hour and the NLS require that pupils should be much more articulate about the processes of reading and writing. In the whole-class and group reading and writing sessions they are actively encouraged to discuss, for example, the way they tackle new words, structure stories and write letters. However, pupils need to appreciate how the discrete elements of writing they daily practise can combine to satisfy 'both personal and social needs'. They must know why they write. This can happen only if teachers themselves realise the nature and function of writing. To achieve this, teachers need to move from tacit to conscious reflexive awareness, so that they, like their pupils, may learn not as objects of a prescribed curriculum, but as subjects of their own.

(King 2000)

Learning in writing

Just as I claimed in the chapter about reading that teachers will fail to make really satisfactory 'reading learning' progress with their pupils unless they have rehearsed and agreed a clearly articulated view about what they believe 'being a reader' means, so teachers also need to possess just as clear-sighted an understanding of those qualities they believe lead to being regarded as 'a writer'. One of the biggest frustrations about this understanding rests in the division of the English curriculum into the separate categories of 'reading', 'writing', 'speaking' and 'listening'. To be properly regarded as a writer means individual pupils have to develop the capability of recognising with great clarity what textual material is about in the first place. If a writer is not well acquainted with the particular devices and structures other text-makers are employing in their texts to convey, to explore or to bring about in meaningful terms, then writing remains a detached, unrelated, almost abstract activity. To enable the growth of this more developed awareness, readers have to be guided through their textual engagements in school as 'potential writers'. Whilst being expected to, and continually tutored in the essential ways of being able to, make personal responses to their reading materials, pupils also need to be supported in considering closely the ways in which the writers they encounter have chosen to structure their texts, have selected the most appropriate vocabulary and language in relation to the text's purpose, and have decided on a particular 'voice' or stance in relation to the matter that is being communicated etc. These issues are not possible to assign simply to activities designated unproblematically as 'reading' or 'writing'; a shift towards more focused, linked textual study and awareness is essential.

The following 'learning outline' with regard to teaching writing can only be regarded as the simplest of starting points; but just as teachers of reading need to have securer guiding principles against which to position their teaching to encourage worthwhile learning, so teachers of writing would also do well to start from the positions contained in the following statements. The issues contained in every one of these statements can be taught, and pupils can improve their skills and make progress in learning in each category, whether in the early, middle or later years of education.

The qualities, or characteristics, of the 'writer' I am recommending are (with a simple explanation of each in parenthesis):

1. A writer knows that writing is a purposeful, controlled, deliberate text-making construct – different from speaking. (Writers need to have a real sense of intent when undertaking any writing exercise, and to be clear why they are attempting to bother to create a written text, because they know that they have to bring into play a large number of criteria to achieve real success.)

2. A writer knows that all writing should be designed to meet the needs of real or imagined audiences. (Is this writing for oneself or for others? What are the 'needs' of other audiences? How can they be met? These external demands might require changes in vocabulary, syntax, approach and tone, amongst other things.)

3. A writer knows that writing should be framed within recognisable text-types or genres. (Writers have to be aware about whether they are, for instance, recounting, explaining, instructing, persuading etc., as the first starting point for their work. They may well be combining different types of text, to fulfil a number of purposes, and they need an understanding of how those combinations can best be effected. Good writers will want to explore textual possibilities beyond the straightforward rules; less confident writers need to be fully acquainted with the straightforward rules.)

4. A writer knows that more precise and effective writing can be achieved through informed grammatical and linguistic choices. (Written texts are devised by the careful selection of words, in an appropriate order rubbing together, performing specific tasks, making effects on their readers. Knowing that one has to be aware of all those features is difficult enough; controlling all those elements simultaneously is hugely demanding.)

5. A writer knows that writing can be more carefully compiled when modelled through reading. (Writers need to know which textual models already exist and what the available writing territory looks like. As readers, they need to understand how texts have affected them or how they have conveyed their messages, to become, in their turn, successful text-makers capable of achieving similar or even stronger effects on their own readers.)

6. A writer knows that writing is a process that can be continually improved. (Writing is a craft. Few writers are capable of achieving the focus of writing, to bring about the desired meaning, at the first attempt. Good writers continually strive to ensure that their fullest meanings are conveyed. Most 'finished'

writing is a compromise by the author, who will have run out of time to hone the writing any more precisely and agrees to its publication at that point.)

7. A writer knows that writing can be used to articulate, rehearse, explore and consolidate ideas, concepts and knowledge. (Writing has many potential functions, and they all require practice and further consolidation. Learning writers need to be shown how writing can be the means by which meaning and understanding can be enhanced and consolidated. Indeed, learning might not be established until the writer has used the medium of writing to articulate what is being thought.)

8. A writer knows that writing can be more successfully prepared and practised through preliminary and ongoing talk. (Writing should not be a solitary activity in English classrooms, but one in which discussion and negotiation are constantly taking place. Learning writers should be continually challenged about the choices they are making and the directions they are intending, both by themselves and with the help of their peers. These collaborative methods need not diminish the final personal independence that should be the goal of this learning.)

9. A writer knows that writing skills can be improved through reflection and self-evaluation of progress. (As in all learning endeavours, the pupil's own self-awareness is crucial. Writers must have a good insight of their own strengths and be capable of identifying areas of necessary improvement, against which to set their writing activities.)

Just as English departments are more likely to be able to articulate and establish programmes for the most effective learning of reading where they have formulated a viable understanding of a 'reader', so English teachers will be more disposed to supporting the creation of properly effective writers having asserted what they collectively agree to be the qualities of a 'writer'. This definition would be the pivot on which all learning of writing should be pursued in the school. In the planning of all writing tasks it should be possible for teachers to refer to at least one of the above 'qualities', to ensure that pupils are frequently reminded of them and regularly practise them. Most secondary schools have whole-school agreements about the requirements to do with writing ('all work will be dated', 'at least one homework a week should be a writing task', 'pupils will be expected to write in black or blue ink' etc.). Virtually no secondary school has a policy relating to the improvement and learning of writing. As a result, pupils are subject to huge varieties of experiences and expectations to do with writing; they fail to gain consistent and progressive support and – unsurprisingly – writing standards doggedly refuse to improve. English teachers might be working hard to bring about better writing, but unless their efforts are sustained and underpinned in all other subjects, any positive effects will be diminished.

Genre-based theories about writing and the work of Halliday contributing to learning in writing

The introduction of the National Literacy developments in secondary schools has received a mixed welcome from English departments. Some have enthusiastically embraced the training materials and suggestions about more systematic lesson organisation, others have been more neutral, 'cherry picking' certain developments, but not signing up entirely. A few have been thoroughly resistant, either because they believe they are already working effectively without extra demands being made from outside, or because they philosophically reject the ideas and background on which the 'strategy' is based.

The Key Stage 3 English programme is not a 'strategy' in quite the same way as its primary counterpart, and the setting for the introduction of such a programme is certainly not as universally common from one department to another as the Literacy Hour was in primary schools. What have never been fully publicised about the secondary programme – which has partly obscured some of its potential effectiveness for a number of departments – are the origins of the programme. Knowing that many of the driving forces behind the work of the NLS derived from the work of Michael Halliday and his theories of the 'social semiotic', and the associated genre theorists such as Gunther Kress, Beverley Derewianka and Alison Littlefair would enable many English teachers to engage more intensively with the materials in ways that could enable learning. Helping pupils to see that language has evolved to fulfil particular purposes, in distinctive social contexts, gives them a surer starting point for thinking about language construction. A huge influence on this way of thinking was the work of the Russian experimental psychologist Lev Vygotsky (1978, 1986), and his valuable insights into the way that language acquisition needs staged, careful support, through what has popularly become known as 'scaffolding', in regard to what Vygotsky termed 'the zone of proximal development'. This process involves the teachers knowing their pupils' current attainment very well, and being able to 'bridge' the gap between where a pupil might be currently situated, and where the teacher wants that pupil to be eventually, in learning terms. Too big a gap between current and potential attainment means the 'scaffolding' will not be adequately supportive to achieve real forward movement; too small and the progress will be minimal; just right and the pupil will have progressed satisfactorily, felt better about the improvement, and will be ready to pursue other gains.

Knowing that the suggestions of the National Literacy team publications have mostly emanated from the sources named above leads to another benefit in learning terms. Part of the understanding of the way language is used, according to the theories of 'social semiotics', is also to explore and better articulate how language is functioning to achieve various purposes. Looking at language in this manner is better known as 'functional grammar', and being aware of this very different approach to grammar teaching and learning, as opposed to the more traditional grammar curriculum, is another valuable step towards taking greater control of language use for pupils. I have explored these matters in far greater detail in *Grammar for Improving Writing and Reading in the Secondary School* (Dean 2003) where I try to 'explore the theoretical vacuum at the centre of the (Key Stage 3) *Framework* materials' (Murray 2004):

> Language is best learned in the context of actual language use. When it comes to grammar, the most important point is to maintain the links between learning to use the language and learning about the language, so that we are not trying to achieve one without the other. This can be managed by locating any early attention to grammar in contexts where the students are using their language with interest and engagement. Then there can be a shift of focus – zooming in and zooming out again – so that the language features are noted without losing sight of the overall context and purpose. Once the students get used to this practice, the teacher can go further, dealing with the grammar more systematically so as to develop a broad framework of understanding.
>
> (Collerson 1994)

Sceptics of these approaches argue their ground on two issues: firstly, that this approach will not bring about the miraculous changes their supporters supposedly claim:

> It is important to remain cautious about the extent to which any of these developments will transform the educational experience or lives of pupils. Centring the writing curriculum on genre and rhetoric will not of itself give pupils access to the audiences they need to begin to influence society; battles are currently taking place to achieve structural control of the Internet which may limit access to it by many less privileged groups in global culture; there are questions to ask about the domination of global language culture by particular Englishes and Englishes collectively.
>
> (Moss 2003)

and, secondly, that these approaches might offer a generic framework, but deny the pupil his/her authentic 'voice' in what is eventually written:

> It is important to realize, though, that this is only one way of thinking about texts and how we read and write them. There are alternatives and the model of language underpinning the NLS, with its emphasis on social convention and appropriateness, does not privilege the writer's voice as something unique and original that is to be encouraged and developed. Nor does the model of language implicit in the NLS appear to be drawn on critical literacy to any great extent so that communications might be understood as ideogically determined.
>
> (Pike 2004)

To which my response would be that it is all very well for pupils to have something to say – and I very much want to encourage them to say it – but they actually need more secure frameworks than they have been offered in the past, in which to formulate what will be articulated. Knowing and being confident with the structure is what the real learning is about; playing with, adapting, personalising and exploring that structure, once confident with it, is what the learning can, ultimately, lead to.

Self-esteem and the learning of writing through 'modelled writing'

To improve as a writer, and to learn as a writer, means that the potential writer has to really want to write. A good many pupils arrive in secondary school already believing that they are not very successful at writing, and they are not enthusiastic about having further attempts. They gain this impression because their teachers write all sorts of advice over those pupils' efforts, and the comments never seem to reduce – or they attained a Level 3 in writing at the end of Key Stage 2! The first matter that secondary English teachers need to address in these circumstances is to convince their pupils that they *can* write, and to set up tasks that lead to success and a subsequent positive attitude.

 To be an effective learner writer, pupils need to be able fully to control what they are undertaking. This means working in a manageable scale. Too many pupils are asked to write pieces of work which are either too long, or are allowed to wander on, eventually growing out of control. There is an argument which suggests that if pupils cannot control and make progress with pieces of work that are relatively short and focused, then they are not likely to achieve those things in longer attempts. If teachers are to be serious about achieving the 'qualities of the writer' suggested above, they will have to adopt an attitude to the setting and supporting of writing through a 'modelled writing' approach which might seem too authoritative to some, but which will establish the sorts of guidelines that enable pupils to 'speak in their own voices', whilst giving them increased security. Pupils will also need to be absolutely clear about the central criteria for success embodied in any piece of writing they are attempting, and to be confident about exactly what it is that their teachers will be assessing.

For a number of writers at the beginning of Year 7, the following suggested activities could contribute to an effective 'learning to write' programme, and also allow the writer to succeed and feel good about what has been achieved. Some writers will, of course, already be utterly secure in this particular level of 'modelled writing', which means that a differentiated set of requirements will need to be planned to ensure the same sort of learning development ensues at an appropriate degree of challenge.

The learning intention might be: 'to know the characteristics of recount texts, and to demonstrate that knowledge by writing a simple example'. The first area of study necessary to contribute to this learning will be the 'immersion' of pupils in relevant examples of the text. They will need some time acquainting themselves, in a carefully staged manner, in active and dynamic ways, with the main characteristics of recount texts. With the teacher's help the pupils should be supported (but not instructed) towards discovering the characteristic features of the genre, e.g. sentences in the past tense, chronological links, active voice, first or third person, variety of sentence structures etc. The teacher could then present (perhaps, in a shared writing context, with pupil suggestions and ideas contributing) an example which becomes the 'modelled writing' template.

An example might be:

> During the summer holidays I usually played with my friends in the park. On most days we would take our skateboards and use the new skateboard centre. I got a lot better as the weeks went by. We had a great time.

The teacher could encourage discussion around the following points:

- despite its brevity, this is a perfect example of a recount text – as it contains most examples of the necessary criteria;
- the purpose of a recount text is to inform an audience, that might not have been present, of what took place at an event etc. – so it requires orientation (allowing the audience to know possibly what took place, where, and who was involved), events in chronological order, and some form of re-orientation to conclude or sum up;
- this particular example comprises: a simple sentence, followed by a compound sentence, followed by another simple sentence, and concludes with a simple sentence;
- this example is written in the first person.

Pupils should then, in pairs or 'writing clubs' or however the writing classroom is organised, be asked to write about a real event in their own lives, in their own words – *but* in *exactly* the same format (i.e. simple sentence, compound sentence, two further simple sentences/orientation, further events linked by time connectives, re-orientation). They could also be required to indicate that they are fully aware of the main characteristics of the genre by text-marking in ways that highlight the component parts – e.g. circling all the verbs in the past tense, underlining the time connectives, writing the first-person pronouns in a different colour etc. In fact, pupils might be asked to write a number of similar examples, until they are fully confident about what they are attempting to create. And they should achieve success every time.

Having become completely familiar and at home with the pieces they have composed, the pupils should then be asked to introduce variations into the formerly straightforward tasks they have completed. For instance, using the model above, pupils might be asked to:

- add one word to each sentence (not an adjective);
- change the first and third sentences to complex sentences;
- introduce an extended noun phrase into any two of the sentences;
- change the word order so the subject does not come first in two sentences;
- change the piece into the passive voice;
- change the tone of the whole text; or
- change the tense of the piece (and discover what that does to the meaning and purpose etc.).

Within the learning context established at the beginning of this unit, any number of variations is possible.

There is good research evidence that this approach to learning writing has substantial positive effects. Roger Beard (2001) cites the work of Mina Shaughnessy (1977) in New York:

> Central to Shaughnessy's analysis is a recognition that syntactical difficulties are signs of unfamiliarity with certain features of formal written English. Shaughnessy reminds us that many of these errors are from attempts to manage more academic and impersonal writing. This kind of writing may require the kinds of formal, complex sentences that are rarely used in speech. She provides several ideas to help students to avoid 'mismanaging' complexity. In particular, she argues that pupils should be helped:
>
> - to behave as writers, using all aspects of the process (composing, drafting, proofreading etc.);
> - to build confidence by providing the supportive and sympathetic contexts for writing;
> - to develop a knowledge of key grammatical concepts, e.g. subject, verb, object, indirect object and a modifier etc.
>
> Shaughnessy stresses that such knowledge is almost indispensable if teachers intend to talk to their students about their sentences.
>
> (Beard 2001)

Writing in this manner, at least in the earliest parts of the secondary school, has a number of important advantages beyond those already stated above. First, pupils are concentrating on the learning; second, there are clear opportunities to explore and discuss the notions of 'audience' and 'purpose' in this concentrated structuring: 'how much information do we have to give to properly inform and involve the reader?'; 'why is this sort of text structured in this way?'; 'What might be the alternatives?' A further advantage is to be seen in the short length of the text. Boys are unhappy about, and not always ready to use, drafting procedures; texts of this scale present no such problems and redrafting is no great effort for any pupil. The work might even be written on a whiteboard, or contained, complete, on the screen of a computer. Repeating the text, in slightly different forms, is also much less of a chore. Checking for spelling errors and punctuation mistakes becomes more manageable, and pupils can learn to proofread closely without being confronted with too much text. EAL pupils, still learning the language, would also be more securely supported through this carefully regulated method of staging their ideas.

Yet all the necessary features for effective learning are contained in this small package. Debra Myhill, who has conducted considerable research in exploring how children learn to write, recommended to a meeting of heads of English that 'weaker writers might be advantaged by shaping whole texts first, then dealing with sentence and word level matters at a later time' (Myhill 2002). Pupils certainly gain a sense of a whole text through this approach, and they are able to understand what a successful text would need to include. Some teachers might still object to these suggestions by claiming that pupils have to be prepared for tests, and to demonstrate their prowess in other assessment respects, by practising writing much longer texts. These claims have real weight, of course. But too many pupils do not 'learn' how to write in the current circumstances. Many do not understand how to pay close attention to the work they are producing, to sustain the necessary concentration needed to submit consistently successful results. If they have not achieved some of those goals working with short, extremely tightly controlled pieces of writing, they will not acquire them by only writing longer, potentially more difficult, pieces.

Other non-fiction text-types can be 'learned' through processing in the same way, and pupils who have mastered these straightforward, uncomplicated textual templates can then be encouraged to mix genres, explaining, while doing so, why they have made those particular choices, to fit the circumstances they are trying to achieve.

Narrative writing can also be practised and developed using similar methods of approach. Pupils might be reading examples of, for instance, action adventure or suspense narrative texts. The Key Learning Intention for the unit might be:

> To know the key characteristics of action adventure (or suspense, fantasy...etc.) texts, and to demonstrate that knowledge by creating action adventure texts of their own.

Pupils would have been closely familiarised with the key characteristics, through careful reading and guidance, and should have identified and recorded them for future reference. A group of pupils in this situation came up with the following characteristics for action adventure texts they had explored:

- concentration on verbs;
- a range of adverbial and adjectival phrases;
- variable sentence/paragraph length – sometimes very short for effect;
- many commas, hyphens etc.;
- unfinished sentences … (ellipsis);
- frequent exclamation;
- breathless, hurried dialogue – or inner monologue;
- a rush of images, without too much reflection.

Considering suspense texts, they found the following features:

- frequent, short, punchy sentences – occasionally one-word;
- adverbs often used to start sentences;
- unusual sentence structures, e.g. 'Before …'/ 'To their surprise …'/'At that moment …' etc.;
- facts/names are hidden from the audience – 'it', 'something', 'the noise' etc. used more regularly;
- characters' reactions often denoted through actions, not description;
- the writer might ask questions;
- heavy use of linguistic effects – personification/metaphor/simile – to create pictures and effects.

Through activities given to identifying these characteristics, pupils will have become far more familiar with the nature of the genre being learned. They should then be supported in writing pieces of text employing the devices that have been identified. This might be initially approached through a 'shared writing' session, where the teacher models a passage or longer piece on the board (or interactive whiteboard, or on a computer network), with pupil contributions that incorporate the known features. Later, pupils should write passages of their own (length, again, depending on past writing success and achievement), consciously incorporating the features now listed on the supportive 'writing frame' that has been compiled earlier. As with the recount passage illustrated above, pupils might be asked to identify – by colour marking-pens or other materials – the actual features they have included, to make obvious the choices they have exercised. Teachers will recognise that important marking and assessment matters have obviously been attended to in this approach. Better still, some time should be found at the end of the activity to invite pupils to go through their own work and explain why they chose to write what they did, and what effects they were hoping to bring about in the minds of their readers.

Talk in the learning of writing

The list of 'qualities of the writer' on pages 108 and 109 contains the indicator: 'a writer knows that writing can be more successfully prepared and practised through preliminary and on-going talk'. Real writing in the real world often involves much preliminary talk and 'exploring around' in collaborative ways. Writing, except of a personal and intimate kind, regularly comes about as writers share their drafts with others, who comment on them or directly suggest alternative or extended ideas. Even acclaimed, published novelists have to share and discuss their manuscripts with editorial staff. Only in the public examination, by which our society sets such great store, are writers expected to work in solitary silence, toiling away over a piece of writing each has to compose entirely alone – more often than not designed to show that some knowledge of one sort or another has been understood.

In the same way that it has been seen as increasingly necessary to articulate to pupils before they learn what it is that they are expected to learn, to enable them to have a clear focus on those features on which that success will be based, so writers need to be encouraged to talk together during the process of writing to share and be reminded of those matters on which they should be concentrating. Pupils, whilst practising their written work, need regular opportunities to explain the decisions they have made about such features as vocabulary choice, grammatical structuring, punctuation and sense. They should become skilled, whatever their ability, from the early days of secondary education, to feel comfortable discussing with, and challenging, their peers about the written material they are composing, are about to write or have recently completed.

Teachers can help pupils gain confidence in this way of approaching writing by establishing in every classroom the notion of 'writing partners' or 'writing clubs'. 'Writing partners' are set up by teachers pairing pupils of reasonably similar writing ability, who should sit together during writing time in the classroom. This partner will be consulted before writing begins, so that the writer has an opportunity to 'rehearse' the piece, and – over time, as confidence and experience grow – be challenged about the ideas expressed. During the actual writing process, time should regularly be made to enable the 'partners' to exchange work and comment on and remind each other of the essential criteria being explored. There might be appropriate occasions when the 'writing partners' are asked to compose together. The concept of the 'writing club' is similar, with the same activities taking place as with the 'writing partners', but involving three, four, five or six (probably the limit) pupils. Teachers need to monitor the progress of these writing organisations carefully, and make adjustments where necessary. They might, too, on occasions, invite pupils to write in other combinations. It would be feasible, for instance, to place a confident writer alongside one or two less-skilled peers for certain tasks in a limited way.

To work in the ways that have been expressed above will mean that teachers will have to change their practices in a number of respects. Planning will require focused writing learning intentions, with criteria for success understood and shared effectively. Writing will need to be seen as a significant learning event, given sufficient attention and a range of contexts in which any learning can be consolidated and embedded in pupils' understanding. Teachers will need to be more participative in writing practices, readier to employ supportive methods, such as guided writing, to model and challenge. Also necessary will be worthwhile follow-up, through considered pupil self-evaluation, in reflective plenary sessions attributed proper value.

Guided writing to underpin learning

An important, potentially powerful, development to encourage the improvement of writing, introduced through the primary Literacy Strategy, was the practice of guided writing. Guided writing should be seen as an essential stage in the writing process. In my book *Teaching English in the Key Stage 3 Literacy Strategy* (Dean 2002), I describe it in the following manner:

> While shared reading and shared writing are probably familiar to most English teachers, the accompanying 'guided' methods for teaching reading and writing are probably new ways of working for most secondary staff...Guided writing allows teachers to involve their pupils much more successfully and directly in their own learning, as pupils have to justify and explain choices they have made in more demanding one-to-one situations. The teacher is able to intervene more potently into pupils' work while it is being composed, or even while it is being planned...Guided writing can offer hesitant pupils ways of setting off on their writing tasks, and is likely to increase their confidence.
>
> (Dean 2002)

Having established the aspect or area of writing to be learned, teachers would probably, first, want to familiarise their pupils with that sort of text in genuine action, by studying already published examples. They would engage their pupils in carefully exploring and identifying the key textual characteristics and listing them, to act as 'writing frames' for subsequent composition. Teachers would then want to demonstrate how to create a new, but typical, example of that sort of text, through 'shared writing', where the teacher goes through a sort of 'out-loud role play', showing the class the many sorts of intellectual problems presented by the construction of that text, and the decisions ultimately being made. They would invite pupil participation in such an activity, but it would usually remain under the control of the teacher.

Guided writing would be the next natural stage as pupils should be ready, at this point in the proceedings, to begin writing their own versions of the relevant text. The class would need to be divided into groups of four to six pupils of roughly similar writing ability. The teacher has to make some difficult decisions at this stage, because it is not possible to work alongside all those groups at the same time, and a reasonable case could be made that they all require attention of some sort. It is more likely that the teachers would mostly choose to support less-confident readers at the very beginning of their writing, joining other groups at different junctures in the writing process. Indeed, one of the strengths of guided writing is that it can be used to challenge and develop pupils' work before they begin writing, at the point of initial composition, part way through the writing, and when the first draft has been completed. Each of those stages raises different and pertinent questions that allow pupils to re-focus on the central issues on which they should be concentrating.

Guided writing is an excellent tool to employ in the learning classroom. The teacher has the opportunity to work closely with the pupils, and to see exactly how well those learners are able to manage the tasks set for them. Using immediate formative assessment, the teacher is then able to adjust the sorts of prompts and challenges being offered to each pupil, to ensure that each makes proper progress in the area of designated learning. The ways of questioning and supporting the pupils used by experienced teachers in guided reading should act as models for the pupils to adopt and employ in their own way as they move through the school. They should themselves be able to work increasingly effectively alongside their peers in future lessons, independently raising the sorts of issues their teachers introduce them to in the early stages, and contributing to an improved supportive culture. Those advocating guided reading also expect the pupils to become more secure about justifying and standing by the sorts of decisions they are making, thus enabling them to evaluate more easily the worth of their writing efforts.

Learning writing from research evidence analysing pupils' writing

It has been the practice in many secondary classrooms during the last few years to list and display for pupils the criteria published in the National Curriculum Orders for English, setting out the writing skills pupils need to demonstrate that they have reached a particular 'level'. These lists are then used to encourage pupils to strive to the next level, by supposedly informing them of the sorts of targets they should be aiming for. According to the Orders, a 'Level 4' writer, the level thought appropriate for a pupil arriving at secondary school in Year 7, would be expected to meet the following criteria:

> Pupils' writing in a range of forms is lively and thoughtful. Ideas are often sustained
> and developed in interesting ways and organised appropriately for the purpose of the

reader. Vocabulary choices are often adventurous and words are used for effect. Pupils are beginning to use grammatically complex sentences, extending meaning. Spelling, including that of polysyllabic words that conform to regular patterns, is generally accurate. Full stops, capital letters and question marks are used correctly, and pupils are beginning to use punctuation within sentences. Handwriting style is fluent, joined and legible.

(DfEE/QCA 1999)

A careful reading of this paragraph soon reveals that it was written by a committee to meet all sorts of political imperatives, but it really has little to do with the developing skills of being a 'writer'. Whilst the compulsory testing of pupils continues at the conclusion of Years 2, 6 and 9, and the 'Levels' awarded are based on the sort of paragraph quoted above, it is understandable why teachers would want to publish for their pupils the yardstick being employed to judge their work. But words such as 'lively', 'thoughtful', 'sustained', 'adventurous' etc. do not offer much of a substantial foundation for learning writers to build upon. To give too much attention to the measures contained in the quoted paragraph is to reduce writing to a limited, functional activity, possibly capable of achieving the attainment of Levels (doubtful), but doing little to improve the commitment and development of real writers.

More effective to help pupils grow as learning writers is to give greater attention to the work typified by Debra Myhill. Debra, with her colleague Alun Hicks, carefully analysed the papers of GCSE candidates 'to investigate the accuracy and effectiveness of pupils' writing' (QCA 1999) in what became known as the Technical Accuracy Project. They used a coding structure to identify different sorts of features in the writing of a huge cohort of pupils, and then reported on their findings in a QCA publication, *Improving Writing in Key Stages 3 and 4*. Debra Myhill also developed the findings in another valuable work, *Better Writing* (Myhill 2001).

Myhill agrees with my claims above that English teachers have never been really clear about the most effective steps in encouraging writing progression:

As a profession, teachers have always been more confident about what constitutes development in reading whereas our descriptions of development in writing tend to have been confined to improvement in accuracy levels and improvement in appropriacy for audience and purpose. To take one illustration for this, the Initial Teacher Training curriculum for secondary English teachers describes for trainee teachers what progression looks like in oracy, reading and writing (*Circular 4/98, DfEE 1998*). The contrast between the specificity of the oracy and reading and reading progression criteria and the vagueness of the writing criteria is stark.

(Myhill 2001)

In contrast, Myhill recommends, with good cause, the outcomes of the Technical Accuracy Project and other subsequent studies of test outcomes, as more likely to identify patterns of progression and development. These are capable of offering teachers greater focus for more secure learning. The following table summarises the sorts of issues on which teachers could be building a more wide-ranging writing curriculum:

Progression criteria in pupil writing	
From:	To:
● heavy use of finite verbs	● decreased use of finite verbs
● little use of adjectives and adverbs	● greater use of adjectives and adverbs
● little use of abstract nouns	● greater use of abstract nouns
● short sentences	● long and short sentences
● similar sentence types	● variety in sentence types
● greater use of co-ordination	● greater use of subordination
● no paragraphs	● paragraph use
● poor paragraph links	● accomplished paragraph links
● opening texts effectively	● ending texts effectively
● writing for self	● writing for a reader

(Myhill 2001)

The strength of these recommendations lies in their intrinsically important qualities; they are not merely offered to assist pupils achieve higher marks in national tests. They also enable learners to shape more focused and better understood targets for improving their writing, support which potential learners require if they are to take greater responsibility in tracking their own progress. The continuum of development contained in these tables also allows teachers to formulate substantial 'learning intentions' of the sort already explored in this book.

Writing questionnaires and writing logs

In much the same way that pupils should be helped to think more critically about their progress as readers, illustrated on page 97, so they should also be urged to ask questions of themselves as developing writers. Starting from the simplest enquiries, teachers could build a searching self-evaluation assessment system to conduct with pupils on a regular basis. Recent research work in the TRAWL (Corden 2001) project in Nottingham has shown that pupils given the opportunities to express a view about their own writing progression adopted a more mature attitude to their work, and were readier to interact with it more purposefully.

The questions do not have to be too complicated. The example on page 122 is an example adopted by a number of primary schools, and could quickly be

Pupil Writing Questionnaire
What sorts of writing do you like writing most?
What sorts of text do you find most difficult to write by yourself?
What could you do by yourself to improve your writing?
What do you need most help with from others to improve your writing?
What improvements will you try to make in your own writing in the next few weeks?
What sort of writer do you think you are?

Figure 5.1 Writing questionnaire

adapted for secondary pupils. Being required to address very straightforward enquiries and articulate their ideas in their own words can help pupils to shape their approaches to their work. Once again, if teachers conduct this sort of questionnaire routinely, it is possible to build up a formative assessment profile of each pupil over time. Those pupils making good progress and feeling increasingly confident can be steered by 'light touch' support, while those who are failing to move forwards in expected ways can be given more direct help relative to the areas of weakness they are identifying for themselves.

Another way of assisting learning writers to become even more competent is to encourage them to use 'writing logs'. These logs are ways of helping pupils reflect on their writing development, and also the means by which writers can practise, play with or otherwise engage with writing ideas in any manner possible, beyond the formal. Writing logs have one important associated difficulty that needs addressing at their introduction; they involve pupils in more writing, when many young people are not willing to write even more than the normal curriculum demands. Nevertheless, most pupils are quite ready to accept the use of writing logs, often because they are able to be used in any manner the writer chooses. They work most effectively if writers use them regularly, but never write much at a time. Just a few words can be sufficient in most circumstances. Having gently edged themselves into the routine of using the logs, a few pupils will begin quite instinctively to write more, and on some occasions use the logs to explore some significantly longer pieces. As with reading logs, the teacher establishes the right to access the logs, by negotiation, but does not 'mark' or assess what is written. It is quite appropriate, however, for the teacher to comment on or question what has been written on certain occasions. The main power of the log is that it urges the writer to articulate any thoughts about the process and to continue to reflect on the writing process at times other than formal writing tasks.

Formative assessment – and 'close the gap marking' – supporting the learning of writing

One of the most alarming findings to emerge from the survey of Black and Wiliam in their influential publication *Inside the Black Box* (Black and Wiliam 1998) is that the traditional forms of feedback on pupils' work, particularly written work, have, in many cases, led to regression of children's progress. This negative effect has been mostly associated with the teachers giving grades for work they have assessed. As Shirley Clarke summarises:

> Comparisons with other children are made all the time in our classrooms so that children are continually aware how their abilities compare to others. This has direct impact on their self-efficacy, or how they perceive their abilities. By giving children feedback about how they have done against the *criteria of the task*, children are released from these comparisons and given breathing space to move forward.
>
> Many secondary schools are now trialling 'comment only' marking, with grades awarded at the end of units, with increased achievement as a result.
>
> (Clarke 2003b)

Whilst many teachers claim that their pupils like having grades or marks attached to their work, it has gradually been realised that they offer a distraction which is difficult to overcome, and demoralises the less able while making the more able complacent. In grading, very little change is possible; those on the top grades usually remain on the top grades, and the order does not move further down. External rewards, such as merit marks or stickers, act in the same way as grades:

Key findings about the use of external rewards indicate that:

- students strive for the reward, not the achievement;
- they encourage competition, rather than co-operation;
- they conflict with deep thinking and investigation (one finds the quickest route to get to the reward);
- they make complacent the more able and demoralise the less able;
- average students get them least; and
- they have short-term motivational gains (effective when classroom circumstances are dire, such as very poor pupil behaviour).

Research undertaken by Clarke and others in Gillingham and Oxfordshire shows that where pupils are given a different sort of supportive feedback, both orally (e.g. 'I know that you are having difficulty with this. Don't worry, I'm going to help you') and in written terms ('These sentences are really successful and meet the criteria – could you rewrite, or add...to these sentences to bring about...?), they are more likely to want to re-engage in the work they are attempting, and ultimately learn more.

Teachers need to indicate features, such as the *three* best instances in the text, where the criteria have been met most closely. Where improvement is thought to be necessary (and these would be limited to very few instances) some suggestion might be made to enable the child to rework that extract in ways that would demonstrate the learning being developed, and be expected to spend no longer than ten minutes on that improvement. This way of responding to pupils' efforts, and assisting them to get as close to the intended learning criteria as possible, is called 'close the gap' assessment. The real point of this approach is to ensure that the pupil, of whatever ability, actually experiences success and can feel at the conclusion of the exercise that the task was relevant and that the pupil took the fullest part. When the pupil can achieve what was the original intention of the work and, as a result, write more purposefully, reflect with some confidence on what he/she has learned from the work, and can feel good about him/herself for what has been achieved, good learning really can be said to have taken place.

Conclusion

> Why is writing so tricky? Because it requires mastery of two conflicting skills: a
> creative skill and a critical skill. The former is of the imagination, the latter of the
> intellect, and they come from different brain hemispheres. To write well, we have to
> employ both with maximum effect.
>
> (Bowler 2000)

Writers need not only something to write about, they also need to be sure that the structures they choose will ensure the exercise has been worthwhile. Too many young people fail to make progress as writers because the canvas on which they are expected to write – the blank sheet in front of them – acts a negative, intimidating force, and they are reluctant to make marks on it. Learning writing means that we have to be able to equip all writers to ask assured but straightforward questions about why they are intending to write, decide on which are the most relevant structures that will be capable of supporting and furthering their purposes, and which words – in relation to others – are the most potent to convey the meaning. To bring about that situation across a sufficiently large number of schools, teachers have to be much clearer about the theoretical choices available to them, and establish programmes that enable their pupils to learn the procedures to employ and the powerful questions to ask of their efforts.

CHAPTER 6

Improving learning in speaking and listening

Making oracy work is often an exciting and challenging part of teaching:

> it is also a complex business, which, at times, involves a degree of risk. To encourage students to talk purposefully and productively in the classroom requires...planning and sensitive intervention by the teacher. It will also entail a degree of handing over control to the students.

> (Howe 1992)

Quite extraordinarily, it took the introduction of the National Curriculum, in 1990, to give the same status to talk in the curriculum, as had traditionally been ascribed to reading and writing. In huge numbers of classrooms before that time, 'talk' had been virtually 'invisible'. While much of the discourse conducted in lessons was spoken, little conscious attention has historically been paid to the medium of the discourse, except in very few instances, and learning in speaking *and* listening was virtually unheard of. Yet, as Alan Howe reminds us in his influential book *Making Talk Work*, Andrew Wilkinson had coined the term 'oracy' in the mid-1960s:

> 'The spoken language in England has been shamefully neglected.' This was the opening sentence of the original edition of *Spoken English* (Wilkinson 1965, with Davies and Atkinson). At that time reading and writing (literacy) dominated the curriculum, both as a means of learning and a method of discipline. A parallel term was needed to give equivalent status to talking and listening, hence 'oracy' was offered.

> (Wilkinson 1990)

and the Newbolt Report into Elementary Education, of 1921, had insisted that 'speech training must be undertaken from the outset' (HMSO 1921). In some ways the Newbolt reference offers clues about the priorities of earlier teaching about talk; it was mostly concerned with a transmission of correctness, and with the sounds and impressions it conveyed, rather than any intellectual development that might be brought about in or through the medium itself.

And if talk, or speaking, has enjoyed far too little regard, 'listening' has been almost totally neglected. Knowing how to pay attention, particularly over sustained periods of time, being able to identify the central matters being articulated from those of lesser importance, and noticing details and nuances that contribute so much to overall meaning are such valuable skills in any reasonable definition of what makes people literate that they require considerable study. But, the reality has been that they have usually been ascribed only the briefest of nods in any English learning programme.

It has become almost a cliché to describe the study of speaking and listening as the 'Cinderella' component of the English curriculum, and, unfortunately, in the same vein, due to lack of space, it has similarly been awarded only a very short section in this book!

> In terms of planning and assessment, time allocation and attention, talk is not being treated as well as reading and writing. Yet the curriculum depends upon talk, and, if educators neglect it, they not only restrict pupils' access to learning, but also fail to equip them as autonomous adults.
>
> (Grainger 2000)

My consultant colleagues who helped me devise the planning proforma on page 60 were so concerned that attention to speaking and listening in the English curriculum were, however, even today, being given such short shrift in general planning arrangements that they insisted that a column dedicated to 'speaking and listening' should be included in the published version as a regular reminder to secondary teachers of their importance.

This situation has to change, however, if effective learning is to be pursued in the future. One of the vital skills, increasingly required of all those leaving school and seeking real success in the next few years, will be their ability to work closely and effectively in groups. This will mean being confident and accomplished in talking, arguing, convincing, sharing, presenting, defending and justifying – and all the myriad other spoken language demands regularly being made by the workplace. Equally necessary will be the skills (note the plural) of listening. Employers, asked to name the essential skills they are seeking in their applicants, name these qualities high on their lists.

What is meant by a good speaker and listener?

Almost inevitably, in relation to this topic, I shall take a similar starting point as was recommended with the establishment of effective programmes in reading and writing. Unless the teachers in an English department or, even better, the teachers across whole school have made some preliminary investigations into, and decisions about, which characteristics constitute the ideal type of speaker and listener, it will be very difficult to outline the most effective plan of action to ensure that all pupils have a chance to acquire those qualities.

The following are offered as examples of what might be regarded as the central principles relating to speaking and listening:

1. Pupils know that speakers can take increasingly purposeful control of speaking engagements in a range of contexts (learners need to be aware of how to direct and control spoken discourses, and to recognise the different contexts in which that control might be exercised).

2. Pupils know that effective speaking meets the needs of particular audiences and contexts (different circumstances and different listeners require different approaches from speakers – knowing the correct manner in appropriate situations is a vital and thoroughly empowering skill).

3. Pupils know that listening skills can be improved by attending in more focused ways to particular oracy events (being aware that it is possible to develop and practise listening abilities is a very valuable starting point for learning to discern all the subtleties of spoken discourses).

4. Pupils know that reading and writing attainment can be supported and improved through talking about, and listening to, the ways meanings are sought and constructed in texts (as someone was once reported as saying, 'I don't know what I mean until I have said what I meant!' Talk is a medium for exploration and analysis of matters in the world, as well as for expression and declaration).

5. Pupils know that learning can be improved through exploring opportunities to articulate what is being considered, in their own words (pupils need to articulate what has been absorbed in their own language and nuances).

6. Pupils know that speaking and listening attainment can be improved as a result of reflecting on the effectiveness of what is said, and on how well listening is conducted (as in all learning, pupils need to be supported in their developing skills of asking rigorous self-evaluatory questions of their progress in these competencies, and how to improve).

Focusing on learning in 'oracy'

For most pupils there is an assumption that speaking does not have to be learned. They have, after all, been communicating through talk since they were very young indeed, and nobody had to teach them how. Reading and writing demand special time and attention, and important skills have to be learned – but anybody can talk. So the problems of talk have to be made clear to pupils, and they must recognise at the outset that there are important lessons to be learned. The issue has to be problematised.

First, they need to see that talk, like writing, has to change from genre to genre to meet different circumstances, purposes and contexts. It is relatively easy to enable pupils to become aware of the different ways they and their friends speak in different familiar circumstances: with each other; with their parents; with teachers, or with other adults in more formal settings. They can also be attuned to the different examples of standard English at work in our culture, from listening to the huge range of announcers, newsreaders, weather forecasters, commentators and 'voice-overs' on television, and the many voices of radio. Being alert to the considerable varieties of 'talk' in these 'natural' settings is an excellent foundation from which to tackle other oracy learning experiences.

Alongside these sorts of awareness-raising activities, pupils should be enjoying opportunities to practise and develop their own range of speaking skills, in real or role-play situations. English teachers can use the context of drama to assist pupils in creating many different worlds, in which characters are able to be explored through the ways they talk and communicate. The excellent *Year 7 Speaking and Listening Bank* (DfEE 2001b), published by the Key Stage 3 National Strategy, offers a good range of situations to explore orally, with much helpful material to help set the scenes of many discourses. As the 'rationale' for the booklet explains:

> It is not enough for teachers to create a range of situations and trust that this will encourage pupils to develop their spoken language. Many of the genres of spoken language necessary for success in school and in the outside world will need to be planned for and taught.
>
> (DfEE 2001b)

and – it should have continued – 'learned'!

A guide to progression, also contained in the booklet, should provide achievable and helpful outlines for a department to build its speaking and listening experiences upon, in ways already suggested in the fields of reading and writing in this book:

> Although much work in speaking and listening revisits and builds on previous teaching objectives, progression across Key Stage 3 is signalled by:
>
> ● developing pupils' ability to stand back and evaluate their own and others' use of spoken language and listening strategies
> ● increasing emphasis on striving for certain effects in more formal situations
> ● greater ability to sustain and develop discussion for particular purposes, including as a means of thinking through issues and problems
> ● increasing ability to appreciate and articulate implied meaning and to listen critically
> ● increasingly complex and unfamiliar demands.
>
> (ibid.)

In his book *Making Talk Work* (Howe 1992) Alan Howe outlines a number of 'kinds of talk'. Pupils need to be aware that talk is capable of being used to:

ask questions	describe	explain	narrate	inform	present
argue	dispute	disagree	discuss	negotiate	clarify
share	analyse	evaluate	comment	report	reason
express and justify opinions		recite and read aloud		etc.	

(Howe 1992)

and goes on:

> this is one of the many lists that could be compiled to show the purposes for which we talk and listen; in one sense the list will be as long as there are human intentions and motivations.
>
> ...Making such a list is a very useful starting point for any group of teachers starting to consider oracy of the first time. Producing such a list will remind you of the multifarious uses to which the spoken word is put, the vast range of possibilities, and thus the need for careful planning.

(ibid.)

Learning in speaking will mean, ultimately, pupils having a keen awareness of the most important areas of talk for a range of purposes, and clear discrimination between the, sometimes, narrow differences of use of some of the words in the above list (e.g. knowing properly what the differences might be between to 'argue', 'dispute', 'disagree', and between those words and 'negotiate').

Dorothy Kavanagh, the Adviser with responsibility for assessment in Oxfordshire, published a paper in 2002 entitled *Assessment for Learning in Practice: Criteria for Observation*, focused on the elements of formative assessment, most of which could be applied to much of this book. Dorothy recognises that good talk can only be properly learned where it develops in supportive surroundings, with good teacher modelling. Specifically, however, she included a section pertinent to the effective talk learning classroom, where the observer should expect to see, amongst other features, the following (with my explanations in brackets):

- hands down – teacher selects pupil to answer (this is to ensure that not merely the enthusiastic are constantly chosen to respond, everybody is expected to participate);
- wait time – all pupils have the opportunity to think before answering (to enable the effective administration of the above);
- pupils encouraged to consult in their group/with a partner in order to formulate and answer (pupils often need to check/rehearse their ideas before expressing them to the whole class);

- teacher involves a number of pupils in the answer to a single question creating the opportunity for discussion – e.g. 'What do you think ... ?', 'Do you agree with that answer ... ?' (this is a version of the methods used by Socrates; the teacher does not express an opinion for each answer but 'passes on' ideas expressed for development by other pupils);

- use of wrong answers to develop understanding (never rejecting answers or putting them down, but skilfully using what has been offered to check knowledge, gain support from other pupils and to help less-confident learners to come to more informed answers);

- appropriateness of questions – fitness for purpose (not just asking one form of question – e.g. closed questions – but having a range for suitable purposes);

- quality of questions, i.e. good question stems, e.g. 'Why does ... ?', 'What if ... ?', 'How would you ... ?', 'Could you explain ... ?' (ensuring that questions expect the pupils to recognise that there are often no correct or single answers, and that questions can encourage genuine exploration in pupils' language);

- opportunities for pupils to formulate questions (if the skills of good questioning, leading to good talk, have been fully learned, the pupils should be capable of raising equally worthwhile questions in their own turn, and will, by that process, be contributing to their developing thinking).

Where talk is valued as an important classroom component, teachers are readier to explore specific exercises designed to further the role of talk in the overall learning processes, as well as a learned skill in its own right. So, it might be more common to see pupils being asked to 'jigsaw' or be acting as 'envoys' or 'snowballing' or taking part in 'rainbow groups'. All these sorts of organisational strategies are the real names of ways in which pupils gain experience of interacting with each other, possibly by representing and summarising the views of others, where talk and listening are required to be used in equal measure.

The Key Stage 3 Strategy has also some useful information to share about making improvements in the listening skills of pupils in the secondary school. The *Literacy Across the Curriculum* materials (DfEE 2001c) include the following statements:

- Listening is an invisible and largely untaught skill.
- Listening is a vital tool for learning.
- The ability to absorb, sift and respond to spoken text is an essential element in achievement in all curriculum areas.
- Listening must be planned for, taught, developed and assessed.

(DfEE 2001c)

and goes on to recommend:

> Effective listening is focused listening leading to a clearly identified response or outcome.
>
> What can teachers do?

- plan for active listening;
- model good listening;
- teach listening skills explicitly;
- teach note-taking to select and transform information and to aid memory.

(ibid.)

Learning as a result of this teaching can be clearly established, if the sorts of 'success criteria' already explored in some detail in the third chapter of this book are applied at the planning stage.

Assessing talk and learning

It goes without saying that the assessment of talk should often be through talk. Pupils should be able to enjoy opportunities to express aloud, and share with others – sometimes teachers, but also their peers – their thoughts on their growing oral skills. Being challenged about how they might have also developed as listeners is also a valid exercise. Yet the assessment of talk has not always readily been addressed or satisfactorily provided in the past.

In many classrooms it is now more usual to see pupils being deployed as specific observers of certain discussion or interactive moments. A pupil, possibly armed with a clipboard and a set of clear criteria, might be purposefully observing what others are saying, and making judgements on what is heard. In some situations, teachers assign roles – such as chair, or convenor, or summariser – to groups of pupils before they begin work, to ensure that the whole class becomes used to acting in each of these important 'talk' jobs.

At the expense of a little ridicule, I would also like to suggest that pupils keep their own records of developing talk, on an occasional basis, through 'talk logs'. I am aware that I have suggested 'logs' of some description, with reference to all the learning contexts that have been explored through this book, and some critics might claim that far too much pupils' time could be taken up with such 'logging'. Some caution and care is, of course, necessary to ensure that teaching and learning have gone on in sufficient degrees, but the reiteration of the potential power of 'logs' is to insist that pupils must become increasingly self-evaluative in considering the matters in school in which they are involved in a learning capacity. If there is insufficient reflection on the identifiable areas of perceived development by the pupils themselves, it can be reasonably claimed that learning is not likely, in fact, to have properly taken place. Therefore, a 'talk log' can be just as effective a way of assessing talk development as those dedicated to the self-evaluation of reading and writing growth and progress.

Finally, the Literacy Team, PAGE, I once worked with in Oxfordshire, devised the speaking and listening observation sheet illustrated as Figure 6.1. It was designed for teachers to take with them as they engaged with groups or individuals in the classroom, and was meant to help them take discrete 'soundings' of speaking and listening activities naturally occurring, and not specifically set up for observation purposes. It is very simple, but it serves a good purpose of reminding teachers that these sorts of assessment opportunities exist all the time, and should be exploited as often as possible. It can also alert teachers to the more usual spoken discourses taking place in the room, and remind them to set up the right circumstances to introduce sorts of talk not so often practised.

Whatever the different devices or apparatus of assessment are eventually decided upon by an English department, they will be almost wholly ineffective unless a solid and substantial learning programme for talk has been decided upon with real insight and understanding in the first place.

Types of talk observed – an *aide-memoire* of things to look for

NAME OF CHILD	DATE
ACTIVITY	

SIZE OF GROUP	GROUP MEMBERS

RECORD OF OBSERVATION

questioning
participating
describing
responding
suggesting

supporting
planning
collaborating
initiating
narrating
instructing

arguing
discussing
reasoning
persuading
conceding

speculating
hypothesising
negotiating
justifying
recalling

reflecting
evaluating

Look for communication strategies:

listening attentively
awareness of audience
mutual encouragement and support

Figure 6.1 Speaking and listening observation sheet. (Produced by PAGE, Oxfordshire)

End words

Education Advisers in any subject are conscious of their extremely privileged position. They are able to see large numbers of professional and conscientious teachers at work in their classrooms, and from their many observation experiences they are enabled to formulate an overview of what they believe are the common practices that make up the subject in action.

I have tried, in this book, to stand back from the matters taking place every day in the classrooms I observe, and to wonder a little more about what are the important linguistic/literacy/literary/English features the teachers I see at work are trying to bring about in their pupils. Yet even with the 'assistance' of a National Curriculum and a National Key Stage 3 Strategy, with a special focus on English, it is simply not possible to identify sufficient common ground to make a secure description.

It was never my intention to offer a solution to this problem, but I wanted to explore the possibilities I think are available to English teachers, if they are prepared to face the crucial questions about what linguistic/literacy/literary/English assurances young people currently in our schools – and particularly those still only in Year 7 or below – really will need to be equipped and successful in the workplace, and to enable fulfillment in their personal lives. It is not enough to claim that the demands of government and Strategy have prevented proper analytic consideration of these matters – or to claim that teachers are not in a position to do anything about answering those questions, and making the most appropriate responses.

English as a subject is at a point of huge potential change. In fact, the possible directions the subject could follow are legion. Those who have direct contact with the subject on a regular basis seem to have lost the will to want to offer reasonable suggestions about its future, partly because they feel they will probably be ignored, or they are too tired. I wanted to establish a few pathways that I believed needed re-opening, and I would be pleased to see a few more teachers picking their way along them.

References

Allen, N. (2002) 'Too much, too young? An analysis of the Key Stage 3 National Literacy Strategy in practice'. *English in Education*, 36(1), Spring, 5–15.

Andrews, R. (2001) *Teaching and Learning in English*. London: Continuum.

Assessment Reform Group (ARG) (2002) *Testing, Motivation and Learning*. Cambridge: University of Cambridge, Faculty of Education.

Ball, S. (1983) 'English and the school curriculum', in Hammersley, M. and Hargreaves, A. *Curriculum Practice: Some Sociological Case Studies*. London: Falmer Press.

Ball, S., Kenny, A. and Gardiner, D. (1990) 'Literacy, politics and the teaching of English', in Goodson, I. and Medway, P. *Bringing English to Order*. London: Falmer Press.

Barton, G. (1999) 'The state we're in'. Book review in *TES*, 22 January.

Bazalgette, C. (1991) *Media Education*. London: Hodder & Stoughton.

Beard, R. (2001) *The Effective Teaching of Writing*. NFER topic series. Slough: NFER.

Bearne, E. (2003) 'Rethinking literacy: communication, representation and text', in *Reading: Literacy and Language*. UKLA/Blackwell, 37(3), November, 98–103.

Benton, M. and Fox, G. (1984) *Teaching Literature Nine to Fourteen*. Oxford: University of Oxford Press.

Black, P. and Wiliam, D. (1998) *Inside the Black Box*. London: Kings College, London.

Bowler, T. (2000) School writer-in-residence programme. London.

Bowring-Carr, C. and West-Burnham, J. (1997) *Effective Learning in Schools*. London: Pearson Education.

Brice Heath, S. (2000) 'Seeing our way into learning'. *Cambridge Journal of Education*, 30(1), 121–32.

Brighouse, T. (2003) website: http://www.cybertext.net.au/tct/context/brighouse/htm

Brindley, S. (1994) *Teaching English*. London: Routledge.

Brooks, M. and Brooks, J. (1993) *The Case for the Constructivist Classroom*.

Virginia, USA: Association for Supervision and Curriculum Development.

Buzan, T. (1988) *Make the Most of Your Mind.* London: Pan.

Carnell, E. and Lodge, C. (2002) *Supporting Effective Learning.* London: Paul Chapman Publishing.

Cazden, C., Cope B. and Kalantzis, M. (1996) 'A pedagogy of multiliteracies: designing social futures'. *Harvard Educational Review*, **66**(1), 60–92.

Clarke, S. (2001) *Unlocking Formative Assessment.* London: Hodder & Stoughton.

Clarke, S. (2003a) *Enriching Feedback in the Primary Classroom.* London: Hodder & Stoughton.

Clarke, S. (2003b) *Shirley Clarke's Thoughts about the Development of Assessment for Learning.* NLS paper for Literacy Consultants.

Collerson, J. (1994) *English Grammar – A Functional Approach.* New South Wales, Australia: PETA.

Corden, R. (2001) 'Teaching reading – writing links (TRAWL Project)'. *Reading Literacy and Language*, UKRA/Blackwell, **35**(1), April, 37–40.

Crace, J. (2003) 'Revision period', *Guardian Education*, 4 November.

Curtis, D. (1993) *Teaching Secondary English.* Buckingham: Open University Press.

Davies, C. (1996) *What is English Teaching?* Buckingham: Open University Press.

Davison, J. and Dowson, J. (2003) *Learning to Teach English in the Secondary School.* London: Routledge Falmer.

Dean, G. (1998/2001) *Challenging the More Able Language User.* London: David Fulton.

Dean, G. (2000/3) *Teaching Reading in Secondary Schools.* London: David Fulton.

Dean, G. (2002) *Teaching English in the Key Stage Literacy Strategy.* London: David Fulton.

Dean, G. (2003) *Grammar for Improving Writing and Reading in the Secondary School.* London: David Fulton.

de Bono, E. (1985) *Six Thinking Hats.* New York: Little, Brown and Company.

DES (1975) *A Language for Life.* London: Department of Education and Science.

DES (1984) *English from 5–16 – Curriculum Matters 1.* London: HMSO.

DES (1986) *English 5–16 – The Response to Curriculum Matters 1.* London: HMSO.

DES (1989) *English for ages 5 to 16.* London: HMSO.

DES (1990) *English in the National Curriculum.* London: HMSO.

DfEE (1998) *The National Literacy Strategy: Framework for Teaching.* London: DfEE.

DfEE/QCA (1999) *The National Curriculum for England – English – Key Stages 1–4.* London: DfEE/QCA.

DfEE (2001a) *Key Stage 3 National Strategy – Framework for Teaching English: Years 7, 8 and 9.* London: DfEE.

DfEE (2001b) *Year 7 Speaking and Listening Bank.* London: DfEE.

DfEE (2001c) *Literacy across the Curriculum.* London: DfEE.

Dixon, J. (1967) *Growth through English.* Oxford: National Association of Teachers of English.

Dixon, J. (1991) 'A schooling in English'. *English in Education,* 25(3), Autumn, 10–17.

Evans, C. (1993) *English People: The Experience of Teaching and Learning English in British Universities.* Milton Keynes: Open University Press.

Fleming, M. and Stevens, D. (1998) *English Teaching in the Secondary School.* London: David Fulton.

Gardner, H. (1999) *Intelligence Reframed: Multiple Intelligences for the 21st Century.* New York: Basic Books.

Goleman, D. (1993) *Emotional Intelligence – Why it Matters More than IQ.* London: Bloomsbury.

Goodson, I. and Medway, P. (eds) (1990) *Bringing English to Order.* London: Falmer Press.

Goodwyn, A. (1992) 'English teachers and the Cox models'. *English in Education,* 26(3), Autumn, 4–10.

Goodwyn, A. (ed.) (2000) *English in the Digital Age.* London: Cassell.

Goodwyn, A. (2004) *Literacy versus English? A professional identity crisis.* Paper to the NATE Conference, January.

Goodwyn, A. and Findlay, K. (1999) 'The Cox models revisited: English teachers' views of their subject and the National Curriculum'. *English in Education,* 33(2), Summer, 19–31.

Grainger, T. (2000) 'The current status of oracy', in Davison, J. and Moss, J. *Issues in English Teaching.* London: Routledge.

Graves, D. (1983) *Writing: Teachers and Children at Work.* Portsmouth: Heinemann.

Harrison, C. (2004) *Understanding Reading Development.* London: Sage.

HMCI (2004) Review of NLS/NNS.

Howe, A. (1992) *Making Talk Work.* London: Hodder & Stoughton.

Jones, A. (1986) 'At school I've got a chance: ideology and social reproduction in a secondary school', in Lankshear, C. *et al. Changing Literacies.* Buckingham: Open University Press.

Jones, A. (1991) *At School I've Got a Chance: CulturePrivilege: Pacific Islands and Pakeha Girls at School.* Palmerston North: Dunmore Press.

Jones, K. (2003) 'Making space for English'. *The English and Media Magazine,* 47, Winter, 8–12.

Kavanagh, D. (2002) *Assessment for Learning in Practice: Criteria for Observation.* Leaflet produced by Oxfordshire County Council Education Department.

Keith, G. (1999) 'Noticing grammar', in *Not Whether but How – Teaching Grammar in English in Key Stages 3 and 4.* London: QCA.

King, C. (2000) 'Can teachers empower pupils as writers?', in Davison, J. and Moss, J. (eds) *Issues in English Teaching.* London: Routledge.

Kress, G. (1995) *Writing the Future.* Sheffield: National Association of Teachers of English.

Kress, G. (2003) *Literacy in the New Media Age.* London: Routledge.

Lankshear, C. (1997) *Changing Literacies.* Buckingham: Open University Press.

Marshall, B. (2003) Quoted in 'Rethinking the Curriculum', *Guardian Education,* 4 November.

Marshall, R. (2002) 'Editorial: revolting literacy'. *English in Education,* Summer, **36**(2), 1–6.

Mathieson, M. (1975) *The Preachers of Culture.* London: George Allen & Unwin.

Medway, P. (2003) 'Teaching and learning the English method'. *The English and Media Magazine,* **47**, Winter, 4–7.

Meek, M. (1994) 'How do they know it's worth it? The untaught reading lessons', in Brindley, S. (ed.) *Teaching English.* London: Routledge.

Mercer, N. (1995) *The Guided Construction of Knowledge.* Clevedon: Multilingual Matters.

Millard, E. (2003) 'Towards a literacy fusion: new times, new teaching and learning?' *Reading Literacy and Language,* UKRA/Blackwell, **37**(1), April, 3–8.

Morgan, W. (1996) *Critical Literacy: Reading and Resources.* Norwood, South Australia: Australian Association for the Teaching of English.

Moss, J. (2003) 'Which English?', in Dawson, J. and Dowson, J. *Learning to Teach English in the Secondary School.* London: Routledge Falmer.

Murray, G. (2004) 'Aiming High: Teflon and Rockets', in *English Drama Media,* NATE issue 1, January, 11–15.

Myhill, D. (2001) *Better Writers.* Westley, Suffolk: Courseware Books.

Myhill, D. (2002) A presentation on 'grammar improving English' to Hampshire Heads of English, 12 July.

Ofsted (2004) *Evaluation of the Primary Literacy and Numeracy Strategies 2003.* London: Ofsted.

Peim, N. (1993) *Critical Theory and the English Teacher.* London: Routledge.

Perkins, D. (1992) *Smart Schools: From Training Memories to Educating Minds.* New York: The Free Press.

Pike, M. (2004) *Teaching Secondary English.* London: Paul Chapman.

Pollard, A. (2003) *Children as Learners.* Briefing paper for Milton Keynes LEA training day, 24 October.

Pope, R. (1998) *The English Studies Book.* London: Routledge.

Postman, N. (1973) *The Politics of Reading.* Harmondsworth: Penguin.

Poulson, L. (1998) *The English Curriculum in Schools.* London: Cassell.

Protherough, R. (1989) *Students of English.* London: Routledge.

Protherough, R. (1995) 'What is a reading curriculum?', in Protherough, R. and King, P. (eds) *English in the National Curriculum.* London: Routledge.

Protherough, R. and Atkinson, J. (1994) 'Shaping the image of an English teacher', in Brindley, S. *Teaching English.* London: Routledge.

Pullman, P. (2002) *Perverse, All Monstrous, All Prodigious Things.* Perspectives on English Teaching Series. Sheffield: NATE.

QCA (1999) *Improving writing at Key Stages 3 and 4.* London: QCA.

QCA (2004) Data relating to the *Monitoring Pupils' Progress* research programme: September 2003–July 2004 (unpublished).

Robinson, M. (2000) 'What is(n't) this subject called English?', in Davison, J. and Moss, J. *Issues in English Teaching.* London: Routledge.

Ruddock, J. (1996) 'Going to big school: the turbulence of transition', in Ruddock, J., Galton, M. and Gray, J. (eds) *School Improvement: What Can Pupils Tell Us?* London: David Fulton.

St John-Brooks, C. (1983) 'English: a curriculum for personal development', in Hammersley, M. and Hargreaves, A. *Curriculum Practice: Some Sociological Case Studies.* London: Falmer Press.

Sampson, G. (1921) *English for the English.* Cambridge: Cambridge University Press.

Sawyer, W., Watson, K. and Adams, A. (1983) *English Teaching from A-Z.* Milton Keynes: Open University Press.

Shaughnessy, M. (1977) *Errors and Expectations: A Guide for the Teacher of Basic Writing.* New York: Open University Press.

Sheeran, Y. and Barnes, D. (1991) *School Writing.* Oxford: OUP.

Smith, A. (1996) *Accelerated Learning in the Classroom.* The School Effectiveness Series. Stafford: Network Educational Press.

Snow, J. (1991) 'On the subject of English'. *English in Education,* 25(3), Autumn, 18–27.

Spufford, F. (2002) *The Child the Books Built.* London: Faber & Faber.

Start, K. and Wells, B. (1972) *The Trend of Reading Standards.* Slough: NFER.

Stoll, L., Fink, D. and Earl, L. (2003) *It's About Learning (and It's About Time).* London: Routledge Falmer.

Thomas, P. (2001) 'The pleasure and the power of the paragraph'. *Secondary English Magazine* 4(3), 24–8.

Traves, P. (1994) 'Reading', in Brindley, S. (ed.) *Teaching English.* London: Routledge.

Tweddle, S. (1995) 'A curriculum for the future – a curriculum built for change'. *English in Education,* 29(2), 3–11.

Tweddle, S., Adams, A., Clarke, S. *et al.* (1997) *English for Tomorrow.* Buckingham: Open University Press.

Vygotsky, L. (1978) *Mind in Society.* Cambridge, Mass: Harvard University Press.

Vygotsky, L. (1986) *Thought and Language.* Cambridge, Mass: MIT Press.

West-Burnham, J. (2003) Milton Keynes Primary Headteachers' Conference, 22 May.

Wilkinson, A. (1965) 'Spoken English'. *Education Review.* Occasional Publication No. 2, University of Birmingham, School of Education.

Wilkinson, A. (1990) 'Introduction: the concept of oracy – retrospect and prospect', in Wilkinson, A., Davies, A. and Berrill, D. *Spoken English Illuminated.* Buckingham: Open University Press.